Charles Backus

Five Discourses on the Truth and Inspiration of the Bible

Particularly designed for the benefit of youth

Charles Backus

Five Discourses on the Truth and Inspiration of the Bible
Particularly designed for the benefit of youth

ISBN/EAN: 9783337191641

Printed in Europe, USA, Canada, Australia, Japan

Cover: Foto ©Lupo / pixelio.de

More available books at **www.hansebooks.com**

ADVERTISEMENT.

THE following Discourses, for substance, were delivered in the place where the writer statedly ministers. What was meant only for a single congregation, is, by the desire of the hearers, now made public. Whether the Book which christians take for their guide, is from heaven or of men, is an inquiry of the highest importance; and in which not a few, at the present time, feel deeply interested from opposite motives. This short summary of the principal arguments in support of revealed religion, is indebted to the defences which have gone before it, and claims no advance in a subject which has employed so many abler pens. It is hoped that this compendious view may be useful to some who have not had access to the large treatises, which have been published on the truth and inspiration of the Bible.

Discourses on Divine Revelation.

DISCOURSE I.

On the Truth of the Scriptures.

2 TIMOTHY iii. 16.

All scripture is given by inspiration of God, and is profitable for doctrine, for reproof, for correction, for instruction in righteousness.

MINISTERS of the gospel are under high and peculiar obligations, in every age of the church, to bear public testimony in favor of the truth and divine original of the religion which they are called to preach. The performance of this duty must lie with uncommon weight upon their minds at the present time; when not a few in America, and vast numbers on the eastern continent, who were educated in the belief of christianity, openly reprobate it, as the offspring of fraud or superstition. It is well known that the disciples of infidelity are multiplying daily, and that they are industriously employed in throwing doubts and scruples relative to the holy scriptures, before the minds of those who have not, as yet, gone over to their side. Whoever has his eyes open to discern the moral complexion of the day, and is friendly to the present and future welfare of mankind, will feel no small concern for the rising generation in particular. Their inexperience, and the warmth of their passions render them liable to become an easy prey to those licentious opinions, which are highly pleasing to the corrupt taste of the human heart.

I REQUEST of you, my young friends, as well as of persons of every age, a candid, serious, and patient hearing, while I adduce some of the leading evidences in support of the truth and inspiration of the Bible, in a more ample manner than I have hitherto done in my public discourses. In prosecuting this design some things will be introduced, which may not, separately considered, be thought very interesting; but I hope it will appear in the final result, that they are necessary parts of the general subject on which I am entering.

If the bible be a piece of priestcraft, or the work of dishonest politicians, let it be given up, and sink into contempt: But if it be from heaven, as we have the fullest evidence to believe, let it be received with all the reverence due to THE WORD OF THE LORD. Not all the art or sophistry of men will be able to overthrow a book that was dictated by infinite truth: And, the guilt of those who make the attempt will be awfully great; for they will be found even to fight against God!

THOSE persons in christian countries who acknowledge the existence of one God, but deny all revealed religion, have adopted the name of *Deists*. They are far from being agreed among themselves, except in the single point of denying the divine original of the scriptures. A considerable number of deists in the last and present century, have appeared as writers against the truth and inspiration of the bible. Some of them were men of acuteness and learning; such as Lord Herbert, the Earl of Shaftsbury, Lord

Bolingbroke, Chubb, Hume, Voltaire, Rosseau, and others. Our country has not given birth to any deistical writer of much note. Mr. Thomas Paine, whose zeal for infidelity is well known, was born and educated in England. On his leaving the United States of America, a few years since, he repaired to France, where he soon found the leaders of a large and powerful nation, as warmly engaged as himself for the downfal of the christian religion, and the propagation of infidelity through the world. Those persons who have read Mr. Paine's "Age of Reason," the first and second parts, have no cause to doubt that he has spoken the language of his heart; for he has gone so far as to utter an oath in a formal manner that he is a deist. On his darling theme he has started little or nothing new, nor has he handled the subject so ably as several who went before him; but in impudence and ridicule he has few equals. It is much easier to deal in confident assertions, or to raise a laugh among the thoughtless, than to offer rational conviction to the mind.

It cannot be questioned that many are fond of calling themselves deists or infidels, because they have heard that some great men have done so heretofore, or are doing so at the present time; though they have never read a syllable that they wrote, and are wholly ignorant of the arguments which they employ in support of their cause. Conversions to infidelity are easily made among those who are void of principle, or are galled by scripture reproofs, or are determined to indulge their lusts. Hence it need not appear strange, that in a season of general licentiousness, many openly renounce the pure religion that came from above.

A LOOSE way of thinking on moral and religious subjects has a strong tendency to blind the mind, and harden the heart. In the history of the New Testament frequent mention is made of the *Sadducees*, a sect who denied a future state, the resurrection of the body, and the existence of angel or spirit. They were among the most bitter enemies of Christ and his apostles. I find no satisfactory proof of the conversion of one of them to christianity. When any have deliberately become unbelievers in the truth and divinity of the scriptures, they have seldom been reclaimed. In most instances they have proceeded from bad to worse, until according to human appearance, they have cut themselves off from hope. God, who hath the hearts of all men in his hand, is able to arrest infidels of the highest class in their course, and subdue them by his grace; but we need stronger evidence than has yet appeared, to be sanguine in our expectations that any of them will be recovered from the error of their way. There is room to hope that such as are infidels through inattention may be excited to careful inquiry, and escape from the snare in which they have begun to be entangled; and that those whose faith is wavering may be settled in the belief that the bible is true and from God. Those who have an anxious desire to be satisfied on so important a subject, will listen with avidity to every attempt to discover the grounds on which the scriptures may be defended, against those who condemn them as fraught with cunningly devised fables.

Pious christians are fully satisfied that the religion which they have embraced is of divine original; but the holy exercises of their hearts are not to be held up before infidels for their conviction. The latter will say, (and they will declare a fact not to be doubted) that they know nothing about the feelings of christian piety. Hence it may be expected that they will consider all who profess such feelings as enthusiasts, and unworthy of notice. Recourse must be had to argument; both to establish the religion in dispute, and to remove objections. The faithful witnesses, though it has been their lot to prophesy a long time clothed in sackcloth, will not withhold their testimony in favor of the oracles of God. Being not ashamed of their hope they will labor to produce such reasons for its support, as may silence, if they do not convince, gainsayers. The glory of God, and the felicity of his holy intelligent kingdom, are directly promoted by the exhibition of truth, however it may " torment them that dwell on the earth." The friends of revelation feel themselves bound to stand up in its defence: The effects of their exertions they leave with God.

The words of the Apostle Paul in the text, addressed to Timothy, a young minister, may lead us to attend to the arguments by which the scriptures are demonstrated to be true and from God. It is added in the verse next following, *That the man of God may be perfect, thoroughly furnished unto all good works:* The meaning of which is, that Timothy by attending to the evidences and design of all scripture, would be completely furnished, as a christian and a minister, for the discharge of every duty to which he should be called.

When the apoftle declares that *all fcripture is given by infpiration of God,* he has particular reference to the writings of the Old Teftament. Thefe were the fcriptures which Timothy had known from a child, as is mentioned in the verfe preceding the text. At the time when Paul wrote this epiftle the whole of the new teftament had not been committed to writing: But fuch is the connexion between its feveral books, and of the whole with the Jewifh fcriptures, that the two teftaments muft ftand or fall together. Whatever diftinct proofs are given of the truth and infpiration of the new teftament, and however convincing thefe may be to a total ftranger to the old teftament, it is well known to every one who has read the bible with attention, that the four evangelifts, the acts of the apoftles, and the epiftles, abound with quotations from, and allufions to, the writings of Mofes and the prophets, on the affumption that they were dictated by the Holy Ghoft. Hence, it has always been admitted both by chriftians and deifts, that the two teftaments are fo interwoven that they muft be jointly eftablifhed, or given up, as the word of the Lord.

The infpiration of all fcripture is not only declared in the text, but its ufe is pointed out : *It is profitable for doctrine, for reproof, for correction, for instruction in righteousness.* It is profitable *for doctrine,* as it directs us what to believe—*for reproof,* as it apprises us of sin and warns us against it—*for correction,* as it recals us from wandering—and *for instruction in righteousness,* as it inculcates all the duties of piety and virtue, with the proper motives to observe them.

In discoursing from the text, at this time, it is proposed,

I. To consider the truth of the scriptures of the Old and New Testament.

II. Explain in what sense the phrase, *Inspiration of God,* is to be understood when applied to *all scripture.*

III. Bring arguments to prove that all scripture is given by inspiration of God.

Under each head it is designed to notice several objections, as we pass along in the discourses.

I. Let us consider the truth of the scriptures of the Old and New Testament.

Every one will easily discern the propriety of considering the truth of the scriptures,

B

or the authenticity of these writings, in the first place: since if they could be shown to be a forgery, their inspiration must be given up; for God will not bear witness in support of a falshood. Besides, we must be satisfied that the scriptures are true, or contain an authentic narration of facts, before we can be warranted to produce arguments from their history to establish their inspiration.

In the part of the subject before us, we are to consider the apparent candor and integrity of the men who are said to have penned the Bible; the circumstances attending the facts they narrate; the corresponding state of the world; and the harmony of the several writers of the scriptures, though living in places and periods remote from each other. To these may be added, the testimony of profane writers, or those who have no claim to inspiration.

When we undertake to examine the truth of the *Pentateuch*, or the five first books of the Bible, said to be written by *Moses*, we have not the advantage of appealing to any cotemporary writer. That there was such a man as Moses, a leader in Israel, has, I think, never been called in question by any deist; and may therefore be taken for granted. He died about fourteen hundred and fifty years before the birth of Christ. There is no profane writer, whose works have come down to us, that lived until more than five hundred years after that period, or about the time that Jehoshaphat reigned in Judah. Herodotus of Greece, is the oldest historian, whose writings have escaped the ruins of time. He did not flourish till more than a thousand years after the death of Moses. That father of profane history did not live until after the return of the children of Israel from Babylon. There are no writings now extant so ancient as the five books of Moses, unless the book of Job be an exception. This is conceded by many of the learned among the deists.

HEATHEN poets and historians have recorded events which reach as far back as the creation. Though they have written in a fabulous strain; it is evident that they allude to facts which were originally taken from the history of Moses. Those writers speak of the happy state of man when he was first created; they represent that he was placed in a delightful garden, and enjoyed all the blessings of what they call the golden age. We also find in those authors an account of the iron age, or the unhappy state of man after he had loft his primeval innocence. Strabo, the Greek geographer, who lived in an early period of the chriftian era, informs that Alexander the Great, who died a little more than three hundred years before Chrift, fent a perfon to enquire into the manners and doctrine of the Bramins, or the Hindoo priefts in India. The meffenger found one of that order named Calanus, who taught him, "That in the origin of nature plenty reigned through all the world. Milk, and wine, and honey, and oil flowed from fountains: but men having abufed this felicity, God deprived them of it, and condemned them to labor for the fuftenance of their lives." Similar reprefentations of man's primitive innocence and happinefs, of his fall, and the bitter fruits of it, have been found in the writings of many of the oriental nations, and in thofe of the Grecian philofophers, who borrowed their theology from the eaft. Thefe accounts were evidently handed down by tradition from fome of the firft chapters in Genefis.

HISTORY and tradition agree with the fcriptures in afcribing to mankind the fame parents, or in deriving them from one pair. The differences in colour have created objections in fome minds againft the Mofaic account of the propagation of the human race. This difficulty is, no doubt, the greateſt that philoſophy can urge. It is certain that climate has ſome influence upon the colour of the ſkin. It is a general fact that the nations who live within the torrid zone are of a darker complexion than the inhabitants of the northern temperate zone. The whites grow darker in the courſe of a few generations by removing into hot climates. It is well known that the Jews, from their attachment to their religion, do not blend with other nations. Experience has determined that thoſe of them who inhabit near the equator for an age or two, are of a darker hue than their brethren who inhabit colder regions for an equal length of time. It will not follow from the influence of climate that men will be exactly of the ſame complexion who have, during any given period, reſided within the ſame parrallels of latitude; for the ſtate of the atmoſphere may be materially affected by high mountains in ſome places, the ſoil, and other cauſes. The Africans on the ſlave coaſt, which lies within the torrid zone, are not equally black. Thoſe who are born and brought up near barren ſands, are blacker than thoſe who have been found in fertile places. The heat of the ſun is much more intenſe on the former foil than on the latter. The manner of living has also an effect on the complexion. Tribes who dwell in dirty, smoky cabins, or huts, are clad with the undressed skins of beasts, and feed on filthy food, are more swarthy than those nations who dwell in convenient houses, and practise cleanliness in their lodging, apparel, and diet. Hence, we may probably conclude why the American Indians have a darker skin than the descendants from the English in the same temperate climate; and why the Tartars, and others, that live at the distance of a few degrees from the north pole, are more tawny than the civilized nations that lie further to the south.

Whether a satisfactory solution of the difficulty to which we have been attending has been hit upon or not, there are so many particulars in which the different nations agree, as to fasten the charge of absurdity on those who deny them to be of one race, from the differences in the colour of their skin. Beside likeness of figure and organs, it has been found that men who are dissimilar in complexion are alike in the passions and appetites both of body and mind; and that by long cohabitation and similar culture the differences between them are not greater than among those who are confessedly of one stock. The similarity between the different nations and tribes of men, is much greater than can be discerned between any two species of animals that fall under our notice. By facts which have been long accumulating, from the reports of those who have most extensively traversed this globe whether by sea or land, the evidence that mankind are all of one race has become decisive.

ALL nations, that have any records remaining, agree in tracing back the original residence of their ancestors at or near that part of Asia where scripture history places them before their dispersion. We can find no account of the origin of nations which will bear examination but that recorded in Gen. x. which concludes with the following words, *These are the families of the sons of Noah, after their generations, in their nations: and by these were the nations divided in the earth after the flood.*

THE antiquity which the Chinese give to their empire, and to the creation, has long been exploded by the learned, as fabulous. The authentic annals of nations, and the state of the arts and sciences, best agree with the Mosaic chronology.

The memory of the flood, which happened in the days of Noah, is preserved in the writings and traditions of all the oriental nations. Marks of the deluge are plainly difcernible in many places. The productions of the ocean have been difcovered in the center of continents, at a great diftance from the fea; lodged in high mountains, and in mines and quarries that lie deep in the bowels of the earth. The face of the globe we inhabit appears to have been rent and torn by fome violent convulfion. The more the furface and the interior parts of the earth have been explored, the higher is the evidence that it was once overflown by the waters of the deluge.

The difcoveries of circumnavigators, have removed the difficulties of admitting that the earth was peopled in all parts from the plain in the land of Shinar, a little to the weft of the Euphrates; on the banks of which river the terreftrial paradife ftood. The art of navigation was imperfectly underftood in the days of Mofes, and long after. It never rofe to high perfection until the polar virtue of the loadftone was known. By difcovering that the magnet would point the needle in the mariner's compafs to the north and fouth poles, with fmall variations, the way was prepared to venture far from the fight of land, and to go on diftant voyages. This difcovery was not made till more than thirteen hundred years after Chrift. Previoufly to that period veffels might be caught by ftorms, or the trade winds, and have been driven to remote iflands, or to this continent. As the mariners had not the means of returning they muft have remained in the places to which they were wafted. Shut out as they were from commerce, and being few in number, they would revert to the rude ftate in which they have been found. The peopling of this weftern continent, the moft difficult to account for of any part of the globe, might have been effected not only by the caufes juft named, but by emigrations acrofs the narrow ftrait that divides Afia and America. It is now known that the north eaft part of the former, and the north weft of the latter are divided by a water paffage of but a few miles in width: and that even favages are furnifhed with craft fufficient for tranfportation.

The boaft which fome infidels have made of being able to overthrow the bible, by improvements in the natural and civil hiftory of the world, and in philofophy, is wholly without foundation. Modern difcoveries lend their aid in establishing, rather than in overthrowing, the Mosaic history; that part of scripture history which lies at the remotest distance from us.

The extraordinary facts narrated in the pentateuch, considered in all their circumstances, are suited to confirm its truth. In this place may be mentioned the plagues inflicted upon the Egyptians, the drying up of the water of the red sea to open a passage through its channel for the Israelites, their forty years journey in the wilderness, the manna rained down from heaven to furnish them with bread, the quails brought round their camp to afford them meat, and the water that gushed out of the rock to quench their thirst. These and similar wonders were wrought to establish the belief—That Jehovah, the God of the Hebrews, was the one only living and true God, in opposition to the polytheism, or idolatry, which reigned among all other nations at that time. Had the story of Moses been false, the enemies of the Israelites would have united in detecting the imposture; and they could not have failed of success. The known attachment of idolaters to their religion, would not have suffered them to be idle spectators of events of such importance. The facts afferted were of a public nature, and therefore muſt have been overthrown had they been falſe. Beſides, a public appeal was made, every year, to ſome of the moſt remarkable of them, by the feaſt of the paſſover, and the feaſt of tabernacles: The former was deſigned as a ſtanding memorial of the ſalvation of the Iſraelites on the night in which the firſt born of the Egyptians were ſlain; the latter was inſtituted to preſerve the memory of the Iſraelites dwelling in tents in their journey through the wilderneſs. Had Moſes been an impoſtor he would not have appointed annual feaſts to keep events in remembrance, which he knew never had an exiſtence. His acknowledged ſagacity muſt have taught him, that on every return of thoſe occaſions, inquiry would have been awakened, which ſoon would have proved fatal to his ſcheme, had it been built on fraud. His conduct had no appearance like to that of impoſtors; who always attempt to hide their deſigns from the public eye, and to avoid ſcrutiny as far as poſſible.

Admitting human nature to have been the ſame in the days of Moſes as now, would it be poſſible for a man to frame ſuch a ſtory as he delivers and obtain general belief, if the whole were a fiction? would he preſume to say, that he went into a powerful kingdom and led out thence more than two millions of people—that the sea was opened to make a paſſage for them on their departure—that their enemies in the purſuit of them were drowned in the ſame channel through which they paſſed on dry ground—that the redeemed nation were afterwards led forty years in a wilderneſs, where they were miraculouſly ſupported from Heaven—and that in their defenceleſs ſtate they were protected from their enemies, who came upon them in great numbers with arms in their hands—I ſay, would he have uttered ſuch a ſtory, in caſe he knew the whole to be a lie, with any expectation of being believed? Moſes could not have indulged any hope of extenſive or laſting credence, if his whole marvellous account were falſe, unleſs he had been a fool or a madman. The ability he diſcovered has cleared him from the imputation of either of theſe characters from the enemies of revelation.

GROUNDLESS ſtories, it is true, have prevailed for a time, but they have always been found to loſe even their temporary credit, when neither fraud nor violence have prevented or ſilenced inquiry. Fond as mankind are of the marvellous, they will in a short time correct their credulity in particular instances, if they are laid under no restraint in examination; especially when facts so notorious as the above are appealed to as proof. Granting, as we must, that the overthrow of one delusion will not cure the human mind of a liability to be deceived again, yet nothing is more true than that the multitude will not hold to any one fable long, when the public evidence which it claims for its support is discovered to be false. Let one now rise up in this country, or in any other, with the professed design of inculcating a new creed, and appeal to facts in proof as public as were those recorded in the Mosaic writings, he would not be believed long, if the facts which he affirmed were not real; provided neither stratagem nor force were employed to blind the eyes of the multitude, or to keep up the credit of the new religion. That the history of Moses has been generally believed, and that for a long time, by most who have been acquainted with it, is not denied by its enemies. We would ask these last, on what principle this faith can be accounted for, if the narration on which it rests be a forgery? If Moses were either artful or tyrannical enough to keep the Israelites in the dark, he could not have enchained the minds

C

of the surrounding nations. The Egyptians in particular, who were at that time the moſt acquainted with ſcience of any nation on the globe, would have exerted themſelves to detect the impoſture, had there been the leaſt proſpect of ſucceſs.

No man or body of men from the earlieſt ages to the preſent day, have taken it upon them to point out the time or the place when and where the Moſaic religion was fabricated, if it be a forgery. Why has not this buſineſs been undertaken? It has not been omitted through a want of abilities for inveſtigation in ſome infidels. Nor have the adverſaries of the Bible withheld their efforts in the preſent inſtance, through want of hatred of Moſes; for no man has been more reproached and vilified by them than he. It can eaſily be told when, where, and by whom, the Mahometan impoſture was framed. Why, I again aſk, has no one undertaken to unravel the plot of Moſes, if his ſcheme be the offspring of fraud? The true anſwer is, that no man of thought and reflection has ever felt himſelf equal to the taſk. The facts of which his hiſtory is compoſed are too glaring to be denied.

The Iſraelites cannot, with the leaſt colour of truth, be conſidered as conſpiring with Moses to establish a false or a groundless story. For though their character, after they were brought under the Sinai covenant, was not so corrupt as that of other nations, it was yet far from being faultless. They are represented as a murmuring and perverse people, and very prone to idolatry. Within a short time after the law had been delivered to them from the mouth of JEHOVAH, with solemn and awful majesty, they, with Aaron at their head, formed a molten calf, and worshipped it, saying, "These be thy gods, O Israel, which brought thee up out of the land of Egypt." While they were in the wilderness they manifested a strong inclination to return to the country where they had been in bondage, and contemplated choosing a leader to conduct them back into that land of idols. Yet perverse as that nation was, and reluctant as they were to the worship of the Lord, they have borne witness to the truth of the history given of them by Moses, and subsequent Old Testament writers. That people bear testimony to the same facts at the present time. Individuals and collective bodies of men wish to have their names handed down to posterity with honor. They shudder at the thought of a disgraceful memory. If we admit that the Israelites would lend their aid to a forgery to render themselves the objects of reproach to their succeſſors, we muſt ſuppoſe that a trait exiſted in their characters, which diſtinguiſhed them eſſentially from all the reſt of mankind that have lived from the creation to this day.

The writings of Moſes carry all the marks of impartiality. He not only mentions the faults of the nation, but his own faults; and proceeds to tell the particular offence which prevented him from paſſing over Jordan, and leading the tribes into the land of promiſe. Do theſe things carry the marks of a diſhoneſt mind? Do they not extort from every candid perſon a confeſſion of the integrity of Moſes?

An objection has been brought forward againſt the truth and authenticity of the Pentateuch, from the paſſage recorded in Numbers xii. 3. *Now the man Moſes was very meek, above all the men which were upon the face of the earth.* Upon theſe words Paine remarks, in his uſual ſtyle and ſpirit, " If Moſes ſaid this of himſelf, he was a vain " and arrogant coxcomb, and unworthy of " credit; and if he did not ſay it, the books " are without authority."

To this objection it may be replied,

1ſt. That from the account given of Moſes, it appears that he was a man of remarkable meekneſs. He bore the inſults of the people at large, and of his brother Aaron and ſiſter Miriam, with a compoſure rarely to be met with even among perſons of real piety. There are certainly occaſions in which a man may appeal to the inoffenſiveneſs and purity of his own character. The reproachful and cruel treatment which Moſes received juſtifies a vindication of himſelf. The credibility of other hiſtorians of far leſs worth than he, has not been called in queſtion from the things they have ſpoken in favor of themſelves, when driven to make a defence againſt the tongue of ſlander.

2nd. The text in Numb. xii. is inſerted by way of parentheſis, and might have been added by ſome ſubſequent writer of the Bible. The account given of the death and burial of Moſes, in the laſt chapter of Deuteronomy, muſt have been added by ſome other perſon. Samuel did not write any part of the ſecond book which bears his name. It is not ſuppoſed that he wrote the whole of the firſt. In the xxvth chapter of the firſt book mention is made of his death. If this event be not an anticipation, but is introduced in the order or the time in which it happened, the evidence is deciſive that he did not write any more of thoſe books than the twenty four chapters preceding. This does nothing towards deftroying or weakening the truth and authenticy of thofe books, unlefs it were fomewhere affirmed in the Bible, that they both and throughout were penned by Samuel. This is no where faid. While the canon of fcripture was unfinifhed, the fucceeding writers might add to the parts which preceded. The manner of removing the difficulty urged from Numb. xii. 3, will be eafily underftood by a comparifon. Let us fuppofe that in fome future diftant period, in a new edition of Doctor Ramfay's Hiftory of the American Revolution, it fhould be added in a parenthefis, or in a note, that Dr. Ramfay was a man of fcience, and of an eftimable character, would this deftroy or even weaken the credibility of his hiftory? The application is eafy to the cafe of Mofes. Some other perfon inferted the eulogy upon him: which in no way affects the truth of what the deceafed wrote, unlefs it be an additional confirmation.

I CONCLUDE this difcourfe with obferving that the truth of the Mofaic hiftory is fuppofed in all the other writings both of the Old Teftament and the New. The evidence we hope to produce in favor of their truth and authenticity, will corroborate the arguments that have been brought in fupport of the truth of the five firft books of the Bible.

DISCOURSE II.

On the Truth of the Scriptures.

---

2 TIMOTHY iii. 16.

A<small>LL</small> scripture is given by inspiration of God, and is profitable for doctrine, for reproof, for correction, for instruction in righteousness.

HAVING in my first discourse, from the words just read, attended to the evidence in support of the truth of the Mosaic writings, I now proceed to consider the truth of the other scriptures.

T<small>HAT</small> the Israelites once inhabited the land of Canaan is as well known, and as universally believed by all sorts of men, as any part of ancient history. Infidels have never denied this, nor that the Israelites were put into possession of that country by conquering its former inhabitants. On that conquest they have raised one of their most formidable objections againſt the inſpiration of the Bible. This objection I ſhall conſider in another place. Tho' in conſiſtency with themſelves, they have rejected the account of the miracles which attended the conqueſt, they have admitted the narration in general which is contained in the book of Joſhua, as true.

AFTER the death of Joſhua followed the rule of the Judges; which was ſucceeded by kingly government. Towards the decline of the kingdom of Judah the hiſtory of other nations becomes more authentic, and corroborates ſcripture hiſtory. After the Babylonian captivity the hiſtory of the Jews is more and more connected with that of the Aſſyrians, the Perſians, the Grecians, and other nations. The return of the Jews from Babylon happened about five hundred and thirty-ſix years before Chriſt. The account given of it by Ezra and Nehemiah, whoſe books the deiſts allow to be genuine, confirms the truth of the predictions of Jeremiah and other prophets to whom were diſcloſed the captivity and return of the Jews, before either of thoſe events took place. Beſides, the writings of Ezra and Nehemiah refer to all the hiſtorical books which relate to the children of Iſrael, from the time of Abraham to the days in which they lived. Thus we fee that the Old Teſtament hiſtory is eſtabliſhed beyond all reaſonable doubt.

In whatever light infidels are difpofed to confider the Jewiſh prophets who lived before the Babylonian captivity, in the time of it, or afterwards, they cannot deny that fuch perfons exiſted, without executing a tafk which they have never attempted, and that is the overthrow of the whole hiſtory of the Old Teſtament. The prophecies and the hiſtorical books are fo interwoven that they muſt ſtand or fall together.

The difficulties which arife from the dates and numbers in the Old Teſtament, are not many; and the few miſtakes in thefe particulars are eafily accounted for. It would be ſtrange if the tranfcribers of the bible, a book much oftener copied than any other in the world, had in no inſtance erred. The Jews, as well as all the other ancient nations, made ufe of letters to exprefs numbers. The figures in arithmetic, with which we are fo familiarly acquainted, are not to be found in the writings of antiquity. They were firſt introduced into Europe from Arabia, about a thoufand years after Chriſt. Several of the letters of the Hebrew Alphabet are very much alike in shape. A transcriber might easily mistake one letter for another, where the similarity between them is very great. An error of this kind might make a numerical calculation very wide from the truth. The Hebrew letter which signifies 4, differs very little in its shape from the one which signifies 200; and the one which stands for 8, from the one which stands for 400. The errors in copies of the scriptures that are of the numerical kind, do nothing towards destroying the truth of these writings. It has never been contended that the transcribers or printers of the Bible, were under immediate unerring supernatural influence. Chronological errors, especially in things of small consequence, have never been considered as subversive of profane history. There is no just cause why any thing should operate as a valid objection against the truth of the scriptures, which is conceded to have no weight in setting aside the truth of any other writing. It may be fairly concluded from the perfections of God, that he will preserve the essentials of any book that has a just claim to inspiration. What need we more?

WITHOUT dwelling any longer upon the truth of the Old Testament, I shall only observe, that when it was closed by the prophet Malachi, about four hundred years before Chrift, the Jewifh church received as authentic the fame books which we have now in our Bible; and admitted no other as canonical.

As we come down to the New Teftament, we fall within a more luminous period than that of Mofes and the prophets.

WE are witneffes of the exiftence of the chriftian religion. However much this may have been, or is now, defpifed, no writer has undertaken to overthrow the belief that a perfon called JESUS CHRIST, made his appearance in Paleftine near 1800 years ago, and that he has had followers in the world, from the time of his entrance on his public miniftry down to the prefent day. The Roman Empire had reached its zenith, and human fcience had rifen to a higher pitch than in any former period when Jefus was born. There are now in many hands the writings of poets, orators, and hiftorians, who flourifhed a little before and a little after his birth. Thefe authors are held in high repute by thofe who have a tafte for the fine arts; and the reading of them continues to form a part of a univerfity education. Evidence can be collected from fome of thofe eminent performances, in fupport of the truth of the chriftian fcriptures.

A QUESTION may arise in this place, in some minds, which demands an answer, and that is, why the testimony of pagans is appealed to in defence of the gospel? To this it may be answered, that their testimony, is the testimony of avowed enemies; which according to common sense, and the approved rules of judging, has no small weight. The Heathens cannot be suspected of attempting to build up a cause which they have ever sought to destroy; or of aiding in the establishment of the facts on which it rests, unless compelled to it by the force of evidence. Let it also be remembered here, that the suffrages of pagan writers are not collected to prove that the scriptures are given by divine inspiration, but for the single purpose of confirming their truth.

THAT the religion of Jesus Christ did exist in as early a period as his followers contend, may be fairly gathered from the writings of Tacitus, the Roman historian, which were published about seventy years after Christ's death. Speaking of the fire which happened at Rome about thirty years after the crucifixion, and of the suspicions that the Emperor Nero enkindled it, he proceeds as follows: " But neither these exertions, " nor his largesses to the people, nor his

"offerings to the gods, did away the infa-
"mous imputation under which Nero lay,
"of having ordered the city to be set on
"fire. To put an end therefore to this
"report, he laid the guilt, and inflicted the
"most cruel punishments upon a set of peo-
"ple, who were held in abhorrence for
"their crimes, and called by the vulgar,
"*Christians*. The founder of that name
"was Christ, who suffered death in the
"reign of Tiberius, under his procurator
"Pontius Pilate. This pernicious supersti-
"tion, thus checked for a while, broke out
"again; and spread, not only over Judea,
"where the evil originated, but through
"Rome also, whither every thing bad upon
"earth finds its way, and is practised. Some
"who confessed their sect were first seized,
"and afterwards by their information a vast
"multitude were apprehended, who were
"convicted, not so much of the crime of
"burning Rome, as of hatred to mankind.
"Their sufferings at their execution were
"aggravated by insult and mockery, for
"some were disguised in the skins of wild
"beasts, and worried to death by dogs—
"some were crucified—and others were
"wrapped in pitched shirts, and set on fire
"when the day closed, that they might serve

" as lights to illuminate the night. Nero
" lent his own gardens for thefe executions;
" and exhibited at the fame time a mock
" circenfian entertainment, being a fpecta-
" tor of the whole in the drefs of a chari-
" oteer, fometimes mingling with the crowd
" on foot, and fometimes viewing the fpec-
" tacles from his car. This conduct made
" the fufferers pitied; and tho' they were
" criminals, and deferved the fevereft pun-
" ifhment, yet they were confidered as fac-
" rificed, not fo much out of a regard to
" the public good, as to gratify the cruelty
" of one man."*

THAT Tacitus was a bitter enemy to the chriftian religion no one can doubt who has attended to the foregoing paffage. It will follow of courfe that this learned pagan adverfary, would have rejoiced at an opportunity to have proved it to be a fable, had it been poffible. His teftimony in fupport of fome of the principal facts on which it refts, could have been extorted by nothing but irrefiftible evidence. We obferve that he teftifies that there was fuch a perfon as Chrift, that he fuffered death in the reign of Tiberius, and under the particular government

---

* Paley's view of the Evidences of Chriftianity, Bofton Edition, pages 33, 34.

of Pilate. He also confirms the account given in the New Testament of the temporary check of the prevalence of the gospel, of the spread of it afterwards in Judea, the original or first spot where it was propagated, and of its extending its influence to Rome; where a christian church was gathered in the same age in which Christ was crucified.

To the testimony of Tacitus might be added that of several other pagan writers. I shall only add that of Pliny the younger, the Roman Governor of Bythynia and Pontus, places remote from the capital. His famous letter to Trajan the Emperor, was written about the same time with the passage adduced from Tacitus; but relates to the affairs of his own time. He speaks of the christian religion, as a religion well known, and as having made very extensive progress in the places under his immediate government. Speaking of the christians, he says, "There are many of every age, and of both "sexes—nor has the contagion of this su- "perstition seized cities only, but smaller "towns also, and the open country."*

PLINY in the same letter mentions the worship of the christians, and gives explicit

* Paley's view, p. 36.

testimony to the purity of their morals. He writes, " That having examined the chris-
" tians, setting aside the superstition of their
" way, he could find no fault; and that
" this was the sum of their error, that they
" were wont to meet on a fixed day, before
" light, and sing a hymn to Christ as God,
" and to bind themselves by a solemn oath
" or sacrament, not to any wicked purpose;
" but not to steal, nor rob, nor commit a-
" dultery, nor break their faith, nor detain
" the pledge."

It is natural to inquire what testimony has been given to the appearing of Jesus Christ, and the progress of his religion, by the Jewish nation, from which he descended as a man. According to the Evangelists Christ's personal ministry was almost wholly confined to that people, and by their influence he was condemned to die. It is certain that the Jews ever since the coming of Jesus of Nazareth into the world, have admitted that he was born in the days of Herod the great—that he entered upon his public ministry in Judea—that he did many wonderful things—that he gained a number of disciples—that by the instigation of their rulers he was put to death—that according to the report of his followers he was restored to life on the third day after his crucifixion—and that his religion had an early and extensive spread. The body of the Jewish nation did not receive him as the Messiah; for they expected, and still expect, a temporal prince under that character. They believed, in the days in which Jesus appeared, that if he were the promised Shiloh, he would have brought them out from under the Roman yoke, and have raised their nation to the summit of earthly glory. The Saviour whom christians acknowledge, declared, both by words and actions, that his kingdom is not of this world; and condemned in a pointed manner, the reigning corruptions in the faith and practice of the Jews. They rejected this illustrious messenger of the Lord of hosts, they charged him with casting out devils by Beelzebub the prince of devils, and pursued him with implacable malice and rancour until they had brought him to the cross. We are not therefore to expect honorable mention of Jesus Christ or of his religion by them. Some indeed of the modern Jews acknowledge that the christian Messiah inculcated many good moral precepts, and justly reproach many of his professed followers with a total want of his spirit; but they consider him still as an impostor. On the whole, we can collect as much evidence from the Jewish nation in favor of the early existence of the christian religion, as could under all circumstances be expected; allowing it to be true.

When we recur to the whole series of christian writers, from the beginning of the christian institution down to the present time, we find that they all proceed upon the general account, which is contained in our scriptures, and upon no other. The ordinances of Baptism and the Lord's Supper, and the Sabbath, have been kept up in the christian church from the time of the Apostles to the day in which we live. The few exceptions found among small and temporary sects of christians, do not affect the general argument, or the usage of the church at large. The foregoing rites considered in this connexion, afford no small proof of the facts which they recognize; such as the death and the resurrection of Jesus Christ, as set forth in the history of the New Testament. We justly consider the declaration of the Independence of the United States of America, as a great and memorable event. Should the day on which it was declared, be marked with peculiar public tokens of respect from generation to generation, will not evidence be fairly collected hundreds of years hence, by those who shall then live, that the political birth of our republic happened on the 4th of July 1776? The application to the subject which this supposition is designed to illustrate, is too plain to be misunderstood.

In further confirmation of the truth and authenticity of the books of the New Testament, we find the four gospels written by Matthew, Mark, Luke and John, and the Acts of the Apostles, are quoted, or plainly alluded to, by a succession of christian writers, beginning with those who lived in the same age with the Apostles, and continuing through all the subsequent periods to the present time. By the works of those writers it appears that the story of the birth, life, ministry, death and resurrection of Christ, and the effects that soon followed, was the same from the first as now. Quotations from the early ages of the christian church, have been made from the Epistles as well as from the historical books of the New Testament. Whoever receives the historical books as authentic and genuine, cannot justly doubt concerning the Epistles; for the latter proceed on the supposition of the truth of the former: as must appear to every one who attentively reads the New Teftament. Its hiftorical books are quoted, or plainly alluded to, by Barnabas, Clement of Rome, Hermas, Ignatius, and Polycarp, as we find by their writings that have come down to us. Thofe fathers, as is generally admitted, were cotemporary with the Apoftles, and were the hearers and companions of fome one or more of the twelve. In the fecond century from the birth of Chrift, we collect teftimony of the kind now under confideration from the writings of Juftin Martyr, Irenœus, Theophilus, Clement of Alexandria, and Tertullian. In the third century, quotations from, and references to, the New Teftament, are numerous in the chriftian writers of that period: among whom are to be enumerated Origen, Dionyfius, and Cyprian. As we advance far into the fourth century, we find the books written by chriftians to be as full of fcripture paffages, as the printed fermons of modern divines; it is therefore unneceffary to name any more chriftian writers under this head. If we be fatisfied by the teftimonies in fupport of the truth and authenticity of the New Teftament, that can be adduced from the firft three centuries, we fhall find nothing to perplex our belief in the ages that have followed.

The force of the testimony which has been brought, is greatly strengthened by the agreement of the several writers with each other, in their references to the books of the New Testament. They also refer to those books as clothed with *divine* authority, and consider the scriptures as the *only* writings which are given by inspiration of God. If it should be said that the writers of the second century were kept from contradicting themselves, or others, in quoting from the New Testament, by attending to the quotations made by the writers of the first century, and that the writers of the third century observed the same precaution it may be observed. 1st. That such an agreement in a forgery, if the gospel be false, among such numbers, in places so remote from each other, and for three hundred years, is without a parallel in the annals of mankind; and since no miraculous evidence is appealed to for the proof of such an unprecedented fact, the objection has no weight. 2d. The christian writers of the first century lived in countries remote from each other. Clement flourished at Rome, Ignatius at Antioch, and Polycarp at Smyrna.

The identity or sameness of the christian story, in every age since it was first promulgated, may be fairly concluded from the early collection of the books of the New Testament into a distinct volume, and the use that was made of them. They were publicly read and expounded in the religious assemblies of the christians who lived in the early ages. Commentaries were written upon them; and they were translated into different languages. Attempts were also made in the infancy of the christian church, to reconcile with each other the different accounts of the four evangelists, as recorded in the copy which we have in our hands.

The use that was made of the New Testament, in the controversies that arose early in the christian church, tends to the confirmation of the subject we are now considering. The several parties appealed to the same writings for proof of their respective opinions. Most even of the heretics acknowledged the whole of the New Testament; and the few who did not, received the greater part of it as true, and of divine original. It is easy to see that the different opinionists who had a respect for the same scriptures, to which they had equal access, would serve as a check upon each other, against attempting any alteration of those writings, had they been so disposed. We argue with certainty in this case, because we build upon the known feelings of human nature. To render the matter plain, let us come down to controversies among christians with which we are acquainted. Should the Presbyterians attempt an alteration of those texts which the Episcopalians employ in support of their cause, the latter would not fail to detect and expose the fraud. The same remark may be made with respect to the vigilance of the Presbyterians, in case the Episcopalians were guilty of the like fraudulent conduct. Were the Pedobaptists, or those who hold to infant Baptism, to add to, or diminish from, the words in the Bible, on which the controversy between them and the Baptists turn, the latter would hold up the designed deception to the world. Were the Baptists to alter the disputed passages, the Pedobaptists would expose the forgery, or erasement. What ever evils have flown from the divisions in the christian church, we discern that good has come out of them in this one respect at least—The preservation of the sacred volume from being corrupted.

In this connexion we may see, that a satisfactory answer can be given to the following inquiry, which we sometimes hear, " How shall illiterate people know that the

" present copies of the Bible, in the original
" tongues in which they were written, or
" in the translation which they have are just?
" As they have no knowledge of those an-
" cient languages, how do they know but
" that they are deceived about the text?"
To this it may be replied—that persons who are unacquainted with the languages in which the scriptures were first written, have no just cause to fear that any material errors have crept into the Hebrew or Greek copies, or into their translations; because learned men of various denominations, and who are, some of them, very wide apart in sentiment, appeal to the same scriptures in their original tongues; and constantly serve as spies upon each other against any alteration of moment, either in the transcribing or translating of them. The present translation of the Bible into our language, is acknowledged by learned men of different denominations, to be done with great judgment and impartiality. The few who have wished to raise an outcry against it, have not been highly respected by christians in general, for their attachment to revealed religion. The present translation was finished almost two hundred years ago.

It is indeed true that a knowledge of the languages in which the scriptures were first written, will be helpful in underſtanding them; becauſe the tranſlators were not wholly clear from miſtakes; and more eſpecially becauſe there are idioms in every language, or peculiar forms of ſpeech, that cannot be completely expreſſed in any other. But the Bible is ſo tranſlated, that no one will be led into any material error by the preſent verſion.

RETURNING from digreſſion, I proceed to obſerve that the ſame hiſtorical books of the New Teſtament, which we have in our hands, were early attacked by the adverſaries of our religion; as by Celſus, in the ſecond century, Porphyry, in the third, and Julian the apoſtate, in the fourth. Theſe learned pagans do not hint at any other hiſtories as received among chriſtians, concerning the life, miniſtry, death, and reſurrection, of Jeſus Chriſt, and the propagation of his religion, but thoſe contained in the four Evangeliſts, and in the Acts of the Apoſtles. Their violent enmity to the chriſtian religion, would have led them to deſtroy or weaken the authenticity of the books which its friends received, had it been in their power. As they never attempted this, but built their objections on the ſame books which are contained in our copies, the evidence is conclusive that the historical records to which christians appealed then, were the same which we now have.

To the foregoing arguments may be added—that many formal catalogues of authentic scriptures were published within four hundred years from the birth of Christ, by his followers, which contain all the books both of the Old and New Testament, that are received by christians, as canonical at the present time.

It is well known to all who have gone far into the inquiry concerning the truth and authenticity of the New Testament, that many spurious or apocryphal writings appeared in some of the early ages of christianity, under the names of the Evangelists, Apostles, and other persons. Such fictions may be accounted for, from the fondness of the human mind to enlarge on a marvellous story that had begun to engage general attention in many places, and from lucrative motives. We have certain proof that those forgeries were never received by the christian church as canonical. They did not appear in the first century from the birth of Christ; in which all the historical books of the New Testament were universally known and received by chriſtians. Primitive chriſtians never appear to have had any doubt concerning the truth and genuineneſs of the four Evangeliſts, and the Acts of the Apoſtles, which contain the principal facts on which the goſpel reſts. Of the apocryphal writings few have been preſerved entire to the preſent time. From theſe, as well as from the fragments of the reſt to be collected from other writers, thoſe ſpurious productions, the moſt of them, are diſcovered to be full of trifling, ſilly ſtories and contradictions, and to be compoſed in a very different ſtyle from the books which chriſtians receive. It is however apparent from all thoſe forgeries, that they allude to the ſame general hiſtory of Chriſt and his Apoſtles which is contained in the New Teſtament. None of the apocryphal writings were ever admitted into the ſame volume with the canonical books, nor into the catalogues of authentic ſcripture that have been publiſhed. They were not noticed by the adverſaries of the chriſtian religion in its infancy, nor were they appealed to, as an authority, by any of the ancient chriſtian writers, in their controverſies with each other.*

---

* The reader who wiſhes to go into a full examination of the truth and authenticity of the New Teſtament, is referred to the authorities which have principally guided the

The differences in the accounts given by the Evangelists concerning the life, ministry, death and resurrection of Jesus Christ create no objection to the truth of their history. Some circumstances are mentioned by one Evangelist which are omitted by another; but on examination it is found that they are all consistent with the general story, and with each other. Differences in history are not necessarily considered as contradictions. Two or more writers on the American Revolution, may mention different facts, and yet their narrations may be harmonious. The genealogies of Christ given by Matthew and Luke are different; but they are reconciled with truth, by considering that Matthew gives the genealogy of Christ in the line of Joseph his reputed father, and Luke traces it in the line of Mary his real mother. The differences in the accounts given by the Evangelists of the Resurrection of Christ, are reconcileable with each other.

The evidence of the truth of the historians of the New Testament is greater, than if they all had mentioned the same facts and

---

writer of these discourses, on that subject, viz. Jones's new and full method of settling the canonical authority of the New Testament, and Paley's view of the Evidences of Christianity. The author regrets that he has not had access to Lardner's Credibility of the gospel history.

no other. In that cafe it might have been objected with more appearance of plaufibility, that they wrote in concert with a defign to make out one ftory, to impofe on mankind. When a number of witneffes teftify to a complicated fact, before a court of juftice, precifely in the fame words and with the fame circumftances, a fufpicion more eafily arifes in the minds of the Judges, of collufion and fraud in the perfons who give teftimony, than when they employ different words, and bring up different circumftances that are reconcileable with the general fact, and with each other, and caft light upon the whole affair.

If any will be fo abfurd as to difcredit the Evangelifts becaufe they narrate events that happened long ago, they muft, to be confiftent reject all ancient hiftory. They muft difbelieve that there ever were fuch men as Cyrus, Alexander the great, or Julius Cefar; for if their exiftence be admitted, credit muft be given to fome of the records of ancient times. We all admit many things to be true of which we have not been eye-witneffes, on human teftimony. If the witneffes be credible, we do not withhold our affent to what they teftify, becaufe the facts they affirm happened at a time, or in a place, remote from us. If we will allow nothing to be true that has not been immediately addressed to our senses, our knowledge will be confined within very narrow bounds indeed.—We of this audience, on that supposition, ought not to believe that there are such places as London, Paris, or Amsterdam; for we have not beheld them with our own eyes.

Infidels, in some of their objections against the Bible, have fallen into modes of reasoning relative to facts, which they would be ashamed to adopt when applied to any other subject. Hence, we have grounds to suspect that they are governed by a wish to prove the scriptures to be false, rather than by the candor which they profess to take for their guide. They urge the supernatural events narrated in sacred history as a sufficient bar against admitting its truth. Mr. Hume, a deist of great subtilty, has labored to prove that experience is the only guide, to be relied on, in reasoning concerning matters of fact. If he mean by experience, what falls under each man's particular observation, he must go all the absurd lengths of discrediting the existence of every thing which is not known either by the immediate testimony of the external senses, or the immediate perceptions of the mind. If Mr. Hume acted upon his own scheme in the sense in which it is now taken, he certainly did not believe in any part of ancient history, except in things daily occurring; such as the rising and setting of the sun, the ebbing and flowing of the tide, the change of the seasons, &c. Nor did he expect that the readers of his history of England, would give credit to a large part of it, unless governed by the credulity which he explodes. If by experience be meant the usual course of events, it will follow that no report which relates to an uncommon event ought to be believed. On this hypothesis, we have no sufficient grounds to believe that King Charles I. of England, was beheaded in the year 1649, or that Louis XVI. of France lost his life on the scaffold in 1793. It has not been usual for kings to lose their lives by the hand of the executioner, after the formalities of a law trial; and as we were not present when either of those monarchs is said to have had his head struck off, we are justified in rejecting the report as a fable. Such absurd consequences as these will follow from the principles laid down by the most subtle deists, for the purpose of destroying the credibility of miracles. If the existence of these is inadmissible, the Bible must be renounced as given by divine inspiration

The portion of understanding which is so equally distributed among mankind, is fully competent to decide on the evidence derived from facts which take place before their eyes. None of the intricacies of abstract reasoning are needed in such cases. This remark agrees with the known sense of all judicial bodies on the earth. To the same common sense I appeal, whether the Apostles and other witnesses of the facts recorded in the history of the New Testament, were not competent judges of the truth of what they assert? If they were, their testimony is to be received as valid; unless it can be set aside from something that appears in their characters, or in the circumstances which attend their narration. No just objection can arise from either of these quarters, when we candidly attend to the case. The truth of the scriptures is fully established by admitting, as all men do when not bewildered by sophistry or prejudice, that credible human testimony is the sole criterion of the truth of facts otherwise unknown. By this plain and approved standard, we are willing that the truth of the scriptures should be tried—We need not fear the result.

THE candor and impartiality of the writers of the New Testament, are too manifest to be denied. They narrate their own faults, without endeavoring to palliate them. This exonerates them from the charge of attempting to impose a forgery on the world. To this they had no inducement. The religion they published condemns falsehood in the strongest terms, and dooms liars and deceivers, in particular, to eternal misery. But had they been so hardened, as to have been in no fear from the judgment to come, they had no temporal inducement to support their zeal for the propagation of the gospel: for by becoming the open advocates of it, they had to renounce the pleasures, the riches, and the honors, of the world, and exposed themselves to meet death in its most dreadful forms. But after all, had they been disposed to deceive mankind with a false story, it would have been wholly impracticable under the existing circumstances. They published their history on the scene of action—they appealed to public facts—and they made the appeal while the facts were recent. Their enemies, who had both knowledge and power, would have unveiled the plot, had their scheme been built on a lie. The rulers of the Jewish nation were, as a body, wholly opposed to christianity, and would have crushed it in the birth had their malice been able to have accomplished its wishes. Had the religion of Jesus been a fraud, it would soon, like other frauds that are detested by those in power, have perished from the earth. We are not to confine the scene to Judea, where christianity was first displayed, it was carried into the lesser Asia, into Greece and Rome and other places, within a few years after the death of its founder. The malice, the learning, and the prejudices of Heathens as well as Jews were exerted against it. Its propagation was not in dark and obscure places, but in the most noted places then in the world. It was too in the day when the famous Roman Empire had brought not only Judea, but all countries of much renown, to bow to her arms, and to pour their riches into her treasury. At the same time that she extended her sceptre over the world, she reigned mistress of the arts. " At the " time when Christ appeared, the Roman " Empire had reached the very meridian " of its glory. It was the illustrious peri- " od, when power and policy receiving aid " from learning and science, and embelish- " ment from the orators and the poets, " gave law to the world, directed its taste, " and even controled its opinions. It was " the age when inquiry was awake and active "on every subject that was supposed to be of curious or useful investigation, whether in the natural or in the intellectual world. It was, in short, such an age as imposture must have found in every respect the least auspicious to its designs; especially such an imposture as christianity, if it had deserved the name."*

THE first planting of the gospel in the world, and its prevalence for so long a time, under all the attending circumstances, if it were a forgery, would be a greater miracle, than any it claims for its support; and would be without a parallel in the history of mankind.

---

* White's Sermons, containing a view of Christianity and Mahometanism, in their History, their Evidence, and their Effects, p. 133, 134.

DISCOURSE III.

The sense in which all Scripture is given by Inspiration of God explained; and the evidence of its divine original from the nature of the religion which it contains considered.

———

2 TIMOTHY iii. 16.

All scripture is given by inspiration of God, and is profitable for doctrine, for reproof, for correction, for instruction in righteousness.

IN the two former discourses from the text, we have attended to the truth of the scriptures of the Old and New Testament. I now proceed,

II. To explain in what sense the phrase *Inspiration of God*, is to be understood when applied to *all scripture*.

By *inspiration* is to be understood, either an immediate communication of facts or doctrines from God, to the minds of the men who were employed in delivering the Bible to mankind, or in directing them what to write, or in securing them from error. They had facts and doctrines communicated to them immediately from God, in some instances, as much as if it were now communicated to us what is transacting, this moment, at the distance of thousands of miles from us. Whenever they wrote any part of scripture they were directed from on High what to record, and at the same time they were secured from error in what they wrote to guide the faith and the practice of mankind. That part of scripture which does not fall under inspiration in the first sense that has been given, falls under it in the two last senses; and hence it may be said with strict propriety, *that all scripture is given by inspiration of God*, and forms an infallible rule of faith and practice.

The meaning of inspiration first given, will be easily understood by a few examples. To Noah was immediately revealed that a deluge would come upon the earth—To Abraham, that his seed should be afflicted by a people in whose land they should be a stranger, four hundred years—To Moses, the deliverance of the Israelites from their Egyptian bondage by his hand—To Samuel, the overthrow of Saul, and the establishment of David on the throne of Israel—To Jeremiah, the seventy years captivity of the kingdom of Judah—To Paul, the Antichristian apostacy—And to John, the duration of the reign of the man of sin, and the principal events relative to the church to the end of the world. Inspiration, in this high sense, is not only employed in revealing facts but doctrines; such as the mode of the divine existence, the character and offices of Jesus Christ, the immortality of the soul, the future judgment, and the resurrection of the dead. Under this head may also be ranked positive precepts, or institutions; whether binding on the Jewish or the christian church.

Those who acknowledge the existence of God, will not deny the possibility of his communicating truth to the human mind in this extraordinary manner; whether by visions, by an audible voice, or in any other way. No person demands credit from others, as having such immediate intercourse with the Deity, unless he evidence his illumination by means as extraordinary as the way in which he received his knowledge. Hence, we may see the importance of miracles to confirm the divine original of the Bible; as will hereafter be considered. We may be under as real obligation to receive as divine what is revealed immediately to others, as tho' it were revealed in the same way to us. The evidence that God hath commissioned others to speak in his name may be so conclusive, as to leave us without excuse in unbelief. Whether the Most High speak to us without, or through, the instrumentality of creatures, his voice is the same, and his authority is equally binding. His right to be obeyed is not founded on the manner of communicating his will, but in his nature, and in our relation to him. Whenever we have certain proof set before us, that the righteous Lord of heaven and earth commands our faith or obedience, we are forbidden to withhold our homage a single moment.

In defining inspiration it was observed, in the second place, that the men who penned the scriptures were directed by God what to write. I need make no exception here for such instances as that of Baruch, and others, employed by the inspired men as scribes; because these last were the mere organs of the men who took them into their service, and pronounced the words which they wrote. If the Prophets, Evangelists, or Apostles, were, in any instance left to their own discretion what to record in the scriptures, these writings could not, with any propriety, be considered throughout as given by inspiration of God; as Paul declares in the text. Besides, if the inspired men were, in any instance, left to their own discretion what to insert in the Bible, we might mutilate it to such a degree, as to render it a very unmeaning book. This has actually been done by some nominal christians. They have professed to believe in the facts and doctrines immediately revealed from heaven; but have considered the subsequent building upon them in the scriptures, as the opinions of fallible men. By treating the sacred volume in this manner, they have brought it down to speak a language which gives very little offence to open infidels. The approach of the former class of persons to the latter is so near, as to render the difference scarcely discernible; and paves the way for their complete union.

In perfect consistency with what has been said, it is admitted, that the Prophets, the

Evangelists, and the Apostles, might have a knowledge of many things inserted in the canon, by their own observation, and the accounts given them by other men. The revelations made to the patriarchs, and the facts handed down from one generation to another, probably were the sources through which Moses was furnished with matter for the book of Genesis. At the same time he was directed by omniscience what to record. This superintending influence of the Holy Ghost, gave the same authority to what he wrote, as tho' it had been immediately communicated to his mind.

The third sense in which inspiration is taken, and that is, securing the sacred penmen from error in what they wrote, is as necessary, as the former ones, to give to the scriptures the divine authority which they claim, in every thing that relates to our religious faith and practice. Whatever doctrines or laws may be supposed to have been given by the Most High, we can have no satisfactory evidence of their divine original, if the men who are said to have recorded them, were not secured from error in committing them to writing.

It may be observed here, that the infallibility of the scriptures is confined to the *re-*

ligious inftruction which they contain. As they were revealed as much for the benefit of the unlearned as the learned, they are not employed in teaching human fcience, or in correcting errors relative to it. Matters of this kind are but incidentally mentioned, and always for moral purpofes. It is wholly foreign to their defign to decide on the difputes in natural philofophy or aftronomy. They leave thefe, and fimilar things, as they find them. They, for inftance, fpeak of the rifing and the fetting of the fun, in a ftile which is familiar to all mankind, and in the fame manner which is ufed, even by thofe who have gone fartheft in the ftudy of the kingdom of nature, at the prefent day.

It is not contended that the perfons who were infpired to write the Bible, were free from fin or error, confidered as *men*; for their faults and miftakes ftand on the facred pages. Even a meek Mofes offended, during the abode of the Ifraelites at Kadefh, when he faid to them, " muft *we* fetch you water out of this rock?" David, who wrote moft of the Pfalms, committed an atrocious crime in the matter of Uriah. Peter denied his Lord and Mafter, and at the fame time horribly tranfgreffed the third commandment. The other infpired men faid and did enough to convince all who have read their history, that they were men of like paffions with others. But, as they were under *the immediate or fuperintending influence of infpiration*, they uttered nothing but what is true; either as matter of fact, or doctrine, or warning, or promife, or threatning, or is, in fome way, related to the defign of the author of the fcriptures, in giving them to the human race. The facred penmen declared facts when they told their own fins. The evangelifts are to be credited, when they inform of the difputes among the Apoftles, who fhould be the greateft in the Meffiah's kingdom, and of their ignorance of its nature. It is as really the defign of the Holy Spirit to have the fins, the follies, and the ignorance, of pious men, expofed, whether infpired or not, as to have doctrines and precepts recorded. It will appear, by a little reflexion, that thofe blemifhes may be improved to enforce the reproof and the correction named in the text. When we fee a Mofes, a David, and a Peter, offend, is not the warning of the Apoftle highly enforced, *Let him that thinketh he ftandeth take heed left he fall?*

THE words and actions of Satan and wicked men are recorded in the fcriptures;

to lay open their characters, to justify God in punishing, and to warn against traveling in the path of his enemies. It is declared of the devil, " That he was a murderer from the beginning; and that he is a liar, and the father of it." We find this character exemplified in the history which is given of him. He came with the malicious design of a murderer, to our mother Eve, and with a lie in his mouth, when he said, *ye shall not surely die.* This first lie that was ever told in our world, has often been repeated since; and the tempter still continues to attempt the ruin of the human race by fraud and malice. Is there a false, subtle, a malicious, and a potent, enemy to mankind, constantly going about like a roaring lion, seeking whom he may devour? And is it not worthy of divine wisdom and goodness, to apprise and warn the human race of his destructive design? How can this be done, without giving to us some knowledge of the disposition of the adversary, and the evils he has introduced? It was certainly a high proof of the benevolence and mercy of Christ, when he said to Peter, " Simon, Simon, behold Satan hath desired to have you, that he may sift you as wheat; but I have prayed for thee, that thy faith fail not."

We have set before us the character of the wicked generation that lived in Noah's time, in Abraham's, and in subsequent ages previous to the coming of Christ, and since; to illustrate the depravity of the human heart, to proclaim the righteousness of God in taking vengeance, and to display the riches of his grace towards the saved. We are moreover warned by such representations against trusting in man, and are counselled to put our trust in the living God. Particular examples of wickedness in persons of different ranks and stations, and some of them under the best external advantages, or under the most solemn admonitions, are adapted to convince us of the obstinacy of sinners, and that the change which is wrought in the renewed is effected by the sovereign mercy of God. A hardened Pharaoh, a blaspheming Rabshakeh, a proud Nebuchadnezzar, a cruel Herod, and a treacherous Judas, stand as so many beacons, to reprove and warn mankind. It is as worthy of infinite truth and purity to delineate such characters, as those of a meek Moses, a pious Hezekiah, a faithful Daniel, a believing Simeon, and an amiable John. When we behold ourselves compassed about with so great a cloud of witnesses, as sacred history points out to us, we have every inducement to lay afide every weight, and the fin which doth fo eafily befet us, and to run with patience the chriftian race.

If any will go about to vilify the fcriptures, becaufe they contain an account of the corruptions of the human race, they betray great ignorance and wickednefs. Such reprefentations as the Bible contains on this fubject, are fo far from fixing a ftain on the character of Jehovah, that, in the connexion in which they ftand, they paint his hatred of fin in the moft glaring colours. No perfon of an honeft heart, and who is tolerably acquainted with the facred writings, can long remain at a lofs what things are held up in them to be imitated, and what to be avoided. The fcriptures collectively may be ftiled *The Word of the Lord*, as they inform us, what the Lord directs us to believe, what to practife, and what to fhun. Their general defign is the fame; whether they are delivered in the form of doctrine, precept, or hiftory.

A large proportion of the Bible is hiftorical. This form of writing is well fuited to engage the mind of the reader, as it communicates inftruction in a pleafing manner. Of the truth of this every one may be convinced, by reflecting on the effects which he perceives from listening to an interesting story. Who can avoid being moved in reading the life of Joseph; the preservation of Moses when exposed on the banks of the river of Egypt, in his infancy; the life of Elijah, and others. The accounts which are given of particular persons in scripture, are not designed to amuse, like a romance; but to afford moral and religious instruction. The history of the birth, life, death, resurrection, and ascension, of Jesus Christ, comprises events of greater magnitude, and higher importance, than any other that have been published in this world.

Scripture history confirms the truth of the prophecies, by conducting us to the fulfilment of many of them. It unfolds the happy tendency of piety and virtue, and the misery that is derived from sin. By the history of the Jewish nation, in particular, are exhibited the effects of obedience, and of disobedience, as they respect communities. Peculiar as was the form of government under which that people were placed, important instructions are given by the divine conduct towards them, to all mankind. The rise and fall of heathen empires, narrated in the sacred writings, proclaim the doctrine of divine providence; and announce, that however nations may be lifted up with their conquests and prosperity, they will, sooner or later, have their reckoning day. The Lord will cause the arrogancy of the proud to cease, and will lay low the haughtiness of the terrible.

The long lists of names which are found in several of the scripture books, are not without use. Among the several purposes answered by the insertion of those catalogues, the two following are obvious, and important: the one is, to confirm the descent of all nations from Shem, Ham, and Japheth; the other is, to evince that Christ, as concerning the flesh, descended from Abraham, in the line of Isaac and Jacob, the tribe of Judah, and the house of David, agreeably to prediction and promise.

Many of the common affairs and occurrences of life are recorded in the Bible. Were all these excluded, we should not have evidence, at least in its present degree, that the sacred volume was designed for the use of mankind. It describes them not only with respect to their moral state, and future destination, but in their various concerns with the present world. Our race, for instance, are represented in the scriptures, as

G

having need of food for sustenance, and raiment for clothing, so long as they remain on the earth. The necessity of these is not diminished by possessing the spirit of piety, or of inspiration. God enjoins in his word a temperate and charitable use of worldly goods, but he doth not require that abstraction from them of the living, which can be found only among those who are lodged in the grave. All temporal enjoyments, including natural life, are to be given up, and literally to be parted with, rather than deny Christ. At the same time it is to be observed, that the sacrifices which are made of earthly blessings to indulge a capricious sanctimony, are not the fruits of evangelical love, but the offspring of pride. Religionists have appeared under the christian name, who have represented the perfection of piety as very much consisting in "neglecting of the body," and in "abstaining from meats which God hath created to be received with thanksgiving of them who believe and know the truth." The Apostle Paul in writing for the cloak that he left at Troas, for the books, and the parchments, shows, that as a man he had the same wants, and might be benefitted by the same outward conveniences, as other men. The insertion of this passage in the scriptures, as well as of other incidents of a like kind, does not appear trifling, after what has been said on the propriety of introducing in the Bible the common affairs of life. It is as really the mind of the author of that sacred book, that such things should be incidentally inserted, as those that were immediately revealed from on high.

THERE are some things which the scriptures declare to be lawful, that may not be expedient under certain circumstances. To a case of that kind the Apostle Paul refers in 1 Cor. vii. 6. *But I speak this by permission, and not of commandment.* Under the head of expediency is also to be placed the advice of the Apostle in the 25th verse of the same chapter, *Now concerning virgins, I have no commandment of the Lord; yet I give my judgment, as one that hath obtained mercy of the Lord to be faithful.* The Apostle is here considering whether it were eligible for christians to marry while suffering persecution, as they were when he wrote this epistle. He gives it as his opinion that it would be better for them to remain in a state of celibacy. He leaves it, however, with individuals to determine for themselves. As **God** hath, by a perpetual law, authorized marriage between the sexes, without the forbidden degrees of confanguinity, and where nothing with refpect to character forbids, the Apoftle could not be commiffioned to deliver a prohibitory precept in the prefent inftance. To the Corinthians, who had written to him to inquire whether it were proper that marriages fhould go on as ufual among their members, it was of no lefs importance to be informed what was left to individual choice, than to know what was pofitively binding on all in other things. The whole church of Chrift is as really inftructed by the text under confideration as by any other. Befides, it is foretold in 1 Tim. iv. that, among the apoftates in the latter times, there fhould rife up thofe who would *forbid to marry.* This prediction has been verified by the decrees of the church of Rome, and of fome other nominal chriftians. The event has therefore fhown the importance of a fcripture paffage, in which an Apoftle declares that God never prohibited marriage in times of perfecution; but that even in fuch feafons he has left it to the judgment of individual chriftians, whether to enter into the matrimonial bond or not. If the foregoing remarks be juft, it will follow, that the text in queftion was inferted in the Bible by the fuperintending influence of the fpirit of infpiration.

When the Apostle says in the beginning of the 12th verse, *But to the rest speak I, not the Lord,* his meaning apparently is, that he was going to deliver something to guide the practice of the church, which had not been before particularly revealed: It is for this reason he declares, " speak *I,* not the Lord." That he is so to be understood, appears from the words which immediately follow in the 12th and 13th verses compared with the 10th and 11th verses. The passages which stand next in order to the clause already cited, are, *If any brother hath a wife that believeth not, and she be pleased to dwell with him, let him not put her away. And the woman which hath an husband that believeth not, and if he be pleased to dwell with her, let her not leave him.* On the conversion of a husband, or a wife, from heathenism to christianity, a question naturally arose, whether the believer was to renounce matrimonial connexion with his or her unbelieving correlate, as the Jews who had married idolatrous wives, were commanded to do, in the days of Ezra. The Apostle forbids divorces on that ground; and the prohibition that he delivers, appears to be clothed with the same divine authority as the one named in the 10th and 11th verses, which contain the following words, *And unto the married I command, yet not I, but the Lord. Let not the wife depart from her husband: But, and if she depart, let her remain unmarried, or be reconciled to her husband: and let not the husband put away his wife.* In this last quotation, the words " not I, but the *Lord,*" refer to what Christ had before spoken on the subject of divorce, recorded in Matthew v. 32, and xix. 9. Mark x. 11, 12. Luke xvi. 18. With the thoughts kept in mind which have been suggested in answer to the difficulties, which have arisen from some parts of the seventh chapter of the first epistle to the Corinthian church, it will, I apprehend, be easy to maintain that the whole chapter claims a place in the inspired volume, as much as any other. If the original penmen of the Bible were, in any instance, left to their own discretion what to insert, it will be impossible to defend against infidels, that *all scripture* is given by inspiration of God, as is affirmed in the text. The Prophets, the Evangelists, and the Apostles, when their matter was immediately revealed from on high, or when it was received in other ways, were guided by the Holy Ghost what to write, and were secured from error in writing. I proceed,

III. To bring arguments to prove that all scripture is given by inspiration of God.

The *first* argument may be taken from the nature of the religion contained in the Bible. In this book the Deity is represented as a spirit, possessed of an eternal, underived, and independent existence; as being every where present at one and the same time; as being infinite in knowledge, and in power, and in every other attribute that is necessary to constitute absolute greatness. JEHOVAH, the God whom christians adore, is not only infinitely great, but infinitely good—He is love. He is the rock, his work is perfect; for all his ways are judgment: a God of truth, and without iniquity; just and right is he. He is the LORD, the LORD God, merciful and gracious, long-suffering, and abundant in goodness and truth. By the word of the LORD were the heavens made; and all the host of them by the breath of his mouth. He gathereth the waters of the sea together as an heap; he layeth up the depth in storehouses. Let all the earth fear the LORD; let all the inhabitants of the world stand in awe of him: for he spake, and it was done, he commanded, and it stood fast. He made the world, and all things therein. He hath made of one blood all nations of men, for to dwell on all the face of the earth, and hath determined the times before appointed, and the bounds of their habitation.

In Him all creatures live, and move, and have their being. The counsel of the Lord standeth forever, the thoughts of his heart to all generations. The Lord hath prepared his throne in the heavens; and his kingdom ruleth over all. The Lord is high above all nations, and his glory above the heavens. Promotion cometh neither from the east, nor from the west, nor from the south; but God is the Judge: he putteth down one, and setteth up another. The Most High ruleth in the kingdom of men, and giveth it to whomsoever he will. He is the blessed and only Potentate, the King of Kings, and Lord of Lords. He is the one Lawgiver, who is able to save, and to destroy. He hath opened a door of hope to a sinful world through Jesus Christ. By his spirit he forms the hearts of sinners to holiness, and prepares them for eternal glory. He is the Judge of all the earth, and will render righteous retribution to all intelligent accountable creatures, forever.* Doth not such a God deserve the devout and thankful homage of man's heart? " O come, let us worship and bow down: let us kneel before

---

* 1 John iv. 16. Deut. xxxii. 4. Exod. xxxiv. 6. Psalm xxxiii. 6—9. Acts xvii. 24, 26. Psalm ciii. 19. cxiii. 4. lxxv. 6, 7. Dan. iv. 17. 1 Tim. vi. 15. James iv. 12, and many other places.

the LORD our Maker! For the LORD is great, and greatly to be praised: he is to be feared above all gods."

THE moral law, delivered from Mount Sinai, consists of ten precepts; the four first of which point out our duty to God, and the six last our duty to mankind. The sum of the whole is, to love the Lord our God with all our heart, and with all our soul, and with all our strength, and with all our mind; and our neighbor as ourselves. The spirit of this law was binding on man from the creation, and every one of its precepts will remain obligatory upon him for ever. What can be more reasonable than that an intelligent creature be required to place his supreme affections upon that infinite Being, who gave birth to him and all things around him? And preserves and governs his workmanship, and is the sum of perfection and blessedness? The other branch of the moral law, which respects our neighbor, is built upon truth and equity. The portion of rational moral existence in our fellow-creatures is of as much worth as ours, and deserves the same regard. Besides, it must follow from our social nature, and the necessity of its indulgence for our happiness, that if we are strangers to holy love, we cannot enjoy society in perfection, or have any of its pleasures long continued to us.

A CODE of laws was given to the Jews, beside the ten commandments, respecting their peculiar government and worship, which was designed to last only until the time of reformation, or the establishment of the New Testament worship; when also the lamp of divine truth was to be carried, as we have seen to the Gentile nations. The peculiar institutions given to the Israelites under the Mosaic economy, were partly adapted to their uncultivated state: such, for instance, was that of the cities of refuge, to provide for the security of those who might undesignedly take away the life of any person. This institution, however, with many others, was designed to teach the necessity of an atonement for sinful man, and of his flying to it as the only way of escaping from the curse of God's holy law. Jehovah taught the children of Israel, for a long time concerning the advent of the Messiah, and the nature of his kingdom, by types and shadows. Particular precepts which may appear to us, under our circumstances, and at our distance of time from their existence, of small moment, were of great importance to that people; as calculated to keep them diſtinct from other nations, and to wean them from idolatrous rites, to which they were ſtrongly inclined. We may add, that in all probability, had the Jewiſh ritual been as ſimple as the Chriſtian, the Iſraelites could not have been kept to the obſervance of it in any tolerable degree, with their general character, without a conſtant ſeries of miraculous interpoſitions: But ſuch conſtant departures from the laws of nature, would, in time, have ceaſed to excite wonder, and the end for which miracles are wrought, would have been defeated.

We may determine from the conduct of infinite wiſdom, that it was not proper that divine revelation ſhould communicate all the light to mankind in the days of Moſes, which it has communicated ſince. The communication of truth was gradual, as appears from comparing the two Teſtaments together. Light was conſtantly increaſing in the Jewiſh church, by the riſe of new prophets, or the fulfilment of former prophecies, until the Sinai covenant was aboliſhed. Comparatively dark as the ancient diſpenſation was, which continued for more than fifteen hundred years, every devout worſhipper knew, that to obey was better than ſacrifice; and that the sum of duty consists in *doing justly, and in loving mercy, and in walking humbly with God.* The Jews were abundantly taught that the Messiah would become incarnate, and dwell among men; and that by his advent light would break forth in greater brightness than in any former period. Hence, the woman of Samaria, who believed in the Old Testament, said, in her conference with Christ, in John iv. "I know that Messias cometh, which is called Christ: when he is come, he will tell us all things."

The manner in which God is to be worshipped, as revealed in scripture, is pure and rational: and contains an admirable display of infinite majesty and condescension. The homage required is adapted to fill the soul with holy reverence, and to inspire it with hope; "For thus saith the high and lofty one that inhabiteth eternity, whose name is holy, I dwell in the high and holy place, with him also that is of a contrite and humble spirit, to revive the spirit of the humble, and to revive the heart of the contrite ones."*

How apostate man may come before the Lord and find acceptance, is a question on

---

* Isaiah lvii. 15.

which the light of nature is wholly silent. It is only in the inspired volume that the doctrine of the *atonement*, which hath been made by the Son of God, is revealed. The mediatorial plan was promulgated early after the apostacy of our first parents, even before they were banished from the garden of Eden for their disobedience. In the fulness of time the promised Saviour appeared in the world, made his soul an offering for sin, rose from the dead, and ascended to sit at the Father's right hand. Through him penitent sinners draw near to God, are delivered from the wrath to come, and are made heirs of eternal life. Whatever difficulties attend the expiatory scheme exhibited in the gospel, we may clearly discern in it, the infinite purity and rectitude of God's character and law—his hatred of sin; and the riches of his grace. These prominent features of the scripture doctrine of atonement, declare it to be worthy of the wisdom of the divine mind; and recommend it in the highest manner to our fallen race. It is only in consequence of the interposition of Jesus Christ, that any of mankind have obtained the heavenly happiness; whether before or since the actual incarnation of the Son of God: " Neither is there salvation in any other; for there is none other name under heaven given among men whereby we muſt be ſaved."

Revelation brings to light the future exiſtence of man, the reſurrection of the body, the future judgment, and the portion of the juſt and the unjuſt in the world to come. Theſe are ſolemn truths; ſuited to deter the wicked, and to encourage the good patiently to continue in well-doing. Nothing ſtamps value on time—on man's preſent life, like the eternal ſtate which is to follow; in which each one is to receive from the righteous judge of the living and the dead, according to the deeds done in the body. The puniſhment threatened to the impenitent is calculated to diſplay the divine holineſs and juſtice; is fitted to their character, and to excite dread. The reward promiſed to the righteous, correſponds only with the temper of thoſe whoſe hearts are united with the God of love.

The piety and virtue inculcated in the oracles of truth, breathe a ſpirit to which the proud and ſelfiſh hearts of mankind are wholly oppoſed. Love to God and man is the root of the graces and virtues, which compoſe the character that meets the approbation of the infinite mind.

THE man whose piety is evangelical, makes an unfeigned dedication of himself to God; and the feelings of his heart, so far as he is sanctified, fully harmonize with the divine law and government. He approaches his heavenly Father with filial reverence, and can, without reserve, adopt the form of prayer that Christ taught his disciples;
" Our Father who art in heaven, hallowed
" be thy name: Thy kingdom come: Thy
" will be done on earth as it is in heaven.
" Give us this day our daily bread. And
" forgive us our debts as we forgive our
" debtors. And lead us not into tempta-
" tion, but deliver us from evil: For thine
" is the kingdom, and the power, and the
" glory, for ever, Amen." This prayer, as one observes, " for a succession of solemn
" thoughts, for fixing the attention upon a
" few great points, for suitableness to every
" condition, for sufficiency, for concifeness
" without obscurity, for the weight and real
" importance of its petitions, is without an
" equal or a rival." The pious man is humble: He feels his absolute dependence on God for good of every kind. He mourns for sin, and begs for pardon through Him who died that sinners might live. While he avoids exercising himself in things that are too high for him, he makes it his study to

know and do the will of God—to maintain sobriety—and to keep alive a devotional temper. Taught that he is not his own, and that he is under the wise, holy and gracious dominion of the sovereign Lord of heaven and earth, he denies himself, he endures afflictions with patience, he encounters evils with fortitude, and resigns every enjoyment to Him who guides the faithful through this disciplinary state. Not intimidated by the frowns, nor allured by the flatteries of the world, he, by divine aid, holds on his course till he finishes it with joy. He daily recounts in his closet, in social prayer, and in meditation, the mercies of the supreme benefactor, and is awakened to gratitude and praise. In solitary devotion he shuns the notice of mortals, shuts the door on the noise and business of the world, and prays to his father who is in secret. Modest and unassuming he is far removed from the ostentatious parade of the ancient Pharisees; who professed religion to be seen of men, and chose the corner of the street, to attract the public notice while they recited their forms of devotion. The real disciple of Jesus Christ does not think highly of his own attainments; but in honor prefers his fellow-christians to himself. Knowing that every moral action begins in the heart, he labors to keep it with all diligence, and is incited to watchfulness. Being a constant witness of remaining inward corruptions, he censures himself in thousands of instances where he stands acquitted in the eyes of mankind.

CHRISTIANITY breathes a kind, meek, and forgiving spirit. The heart of him who is under its influence is moved at the cry of distress, and his hand is open, according to his ability, to supply the wants of the poor, and to alleviate the miseries of the wretched. In almsgiving he does not sound a trumpet before him, but, as much as possible, dispenses his benefactions in secret. He does not indulge envy, malice, or revenge; but strives to overcome evil with good. He is not under the government of those passions which chastity forbids, but looks with abhorrence upon them; as unfitting the mind for pure enjoyment, and the inlet of innumerable evils to the human race. In his intercourse with mankind, he is just in his dealings, faithful to his engagements, and the fulfilment of the duties of his particular trust. He bears on his mind and heart the words of Christ, in Matthew vii. 12. *Therefore all things whatsoever ye would that men should do to you, do ye even so to them: for this is the law and the prophets*. The fpirit of chriftian virtue tends to the diffufion of peace and happinefs thro' families, focieties, and the great brotherhood of man. How far do the moſt improved in the family of Chriſt on the earth, fall ſhort of the pattern exhibited by his doctrine and example! But imperfect as his followers are, the internal beauty of the gofpel remains; and its influences upon them fpeak in its praife. It is a part of its peculiar glory, to train up men from fmall beginnings of holinefs to a ſtate of perfect purity and joy.

In a review of the argument in fupport of the infpiration of the Bible from the religion it contains, it is natural to inquire whence came fuch a fcheme of faith and practice? Where did Mofes and the Ifraelites get fuch ideas of Deity as are exhibited in the Old Teſtament? They did not derive them from Egypt; for that kingdom was overrun with idolatry during their abode in it. They could not acquire their theology from any of the nations that bordered on Egypt, or Canaan, or from any other then on the earth; for they were all involved in the darknefs of paganifm, and remained in that ſtate until the days of the Apoſtles. Hence, the facred writers who followed Mofes could not have been enlightened in the

knowledge and worship of the one living and true God, by any men on the earth. It is well known that the heathens hold to a vast number of gods. Athens—learned and polite Athens, is said to have acknowledged deities to the number of thirty thousand. The objects to which pagans have paid divine homage, were, many of them fabricated by art; and to all their gods have been attributed sensual appetites, and passions, or affections, unworthy of divinity. They are represented by those who adore them, as engaged in the amours of the libidinous, and as parties in the quarrels of proud and malicious men. Many of the heathen rituals enjoined the offering of human sacrifices; and others encouraged drunkenness, obscenity, and whoredom. Some of the wiser men among the pagans have confessed the need of a supernatural revelation, to teach mankind how to worship the Deity aright. Modern infidels have gloried in the wisdom of a heathen Socrates. He was indeed one of the most deserving characters that can be found in the annals of pagan antiquity. This renowned philosopher, " meeting Al-
" cibiades, who was going to the temple to
" pray, proves to him that he knew not how
" to perform that duty aright, and that
" therefore it was not safe for him to do

" it; but that he should wait for a divine
" instructor to teach him how to behave
" both towards the gods and men; and that
" it was necessary that God should scatter
" the darkness which covered his soul, that
" he might be put in a condition to dis-
" cern good and evil."* Were Socrates a-
gain to appear in the world, with his former belief, he would disown those as his disciples, who boast of his knowledge, as a proof of the sufficiency of human reason to direct mankind in the duties of piety and benevolence. But to return, I further ask, whence came the doctrine of the atonement, of the resurrection, and of the future state of rewards and punishments, as contained in the scriptures? Who communicated the piety and virtue which are described and recommended in these writings? No one who is acquainted with the pagan theology, can, with the least colour of reason, pretend that the religion of the Bible was copied from the religion of idolaters. Does the spirit of the book, whose divine original I am endeavoring to maintain, carry the air of human invention? Good men would not impose a forgery on the world for truth.

---

* Leland's View of deistical writers, in 2 vol. page 11th of vol. I.

Bad men could not have a single motive to prompt them to devise such a scheme of faith and practice: For had they knowledge equal to the task, they would not have employed it in the establishment of a plan, which exposes and condemns them in its whole design. The drift of all the sacred books from Genesis to the Revelation of John, is directly in the face of fraud and every species of iniquity, both public and private. Besides, the humble, pious, and disinterested, spirit of the gospel, has not one charm to the unholy and the selfish. To admit that such characters as these last would invent such a religion, if competent in point of ability, would be as absurd as to grant, that a malicious man will direct every effort to promote the good of the one he inveterately hates, or that a selfish man will act from disinterested motives, or that a covetous man will make it his whole aim to be liberal.

THERE is no answer to be given to the question, whence came the religion contained in the Bible? that can satisfy a candid reflecting mind, but this, IT CAME FROM GOD! And therefore the men who announced it to the world, spake as they were moved by the Holy Ghost.

DISCOURSE IV.

Objections raised against the commands for borrowing of the Egyptians, and the extirpation of the Canaanites, answered; and the evidence of Miracles considered.

2 TIMOTHY iii. 16.

All scripture is given by inspiration of God, and is profitable for doctrine, for reproof, for correction, for instruction in righteousness.

IN the conclusion of the last discourse, was introduced an argument in support of the inspiration of the Bible, taken from the nature of the religion it contains. Against its pure and benevolent nature several objections have been brought. I shall, in this place, attend to two, raised against the morality of certain parts of the Old Testament, which are delivered under the sanction of a divine precept. The difficulties I have in view, are those which have been started from the commands which Jehovah gave to the children of Israel, to borrow of the Egyptians, and to cut off the Canaanites.

The first of these injunctions is recorded in Exodus xi. 2. *Speak now in the ears of the people, and let every man borrow of his neighbor, and every woman of her neighbor, jewels of silver, and jewels of gold.* The Israelites practised agreeably to the direction received, on the night in which they left Egypt; as we learn from Exodus xii. 35, 36. "And the children of Israel did according to the word of Moses; and they borrowed of the Egyptians jewels of silver, and jewels of gold, and raiment. And the Lord gave the people favor in the sight of the Egyptians, so that they lent unto them such things as they required; and they spoiled the Egyptians." It has been said that this conduct is not reconcileable with truth or justice, and therefore God could not authorize it as Moses declares; and that by certain consequence it must follow, that the book which contains the licence for such practice cannot be given by divine inspiration. To remove this objection it may be observed,

1st. That the Egyptians had long held the Israelites in cruel bondage, and, in point of juſtice, owed them a large compenſation in property, for their ſervice; and to a higher amount than they actually received.

2dly. The Hebrew verb rendered *borrow*, in the foregoing paſſages, literally ſignifies to *aſk*; and is ſo tranſlated in general.* According to this verſion the difficulty is at once removed. The Iſraelites had certainly an equitable claim on the Egyptians their oppreſſors; and on that ground might aſk of them precious jewels and raiment.

3dly. The difficulty does not appear inſurmountable, if we allow the word *borrow* to ſtand, as in the Bible which we have in our hands. The Iſraelites were not holden, by any engagement of theirs to return the loan, until they ſhould reach Mount Sinai, where they were to worſhip Jehovah their deliverer. But previouſly to their arrival at that place, Pharaoh and his hoſt purſued them with a hoſtile deſign. The Lord interpoſed and cut off the king with his army, by drowning them in the red ſea. The Iſraelites could be juſtified in retaining the jewels and the raiment in their poſſeſſion, as the property of a public enemy. Under the

---

* Gen. xxxii. 29. Deut. iv. 32. xxxii. 7. Joſhua iv. 6. Judges xviii. 5. 1 Sam. xii. 19. Pſalm ii. 8. Iſaiah vii. 11.

existing circumstances, what they first received in a way of loan, became spoil, and hence their obligation to return it ceased.

4thly. Since the earth is the Lord's and the fulness thereof, he may transfer his gifts, in an extraordinary, as well as in an ordinary, manner, if he please. The plagues inflicted on the Egyptians in their own country, and their overthrow at the red sea, served as so many miraculous attestations in support of the equitable claim of the people whom they had so long oppressed, upon their goods; and authorized the redeemed nation in holding the jewels and the raiment, which had been put into their hands. None can justly plead the case we have been considering as a precedent to redress their wrongs in the same way, unless they can produce miracles in their justification, as convincing as those that were wrought for the deliverance of the Israelites from their Egyptian bondage. The Lord brought them forth with a mighty hand, and with an outstretched arm, and with great terribleness, and with signs, and with wonders. The wrath of Jehovah was awfully displayed in the punishment of the Egyptians. Ruin was spread over the face of their land, mourning for the death of their first-born was heard from every houfe, and they were fpoiled of their choiceft treafures. The Lord brought forth his people " with filver and gold; and there was not one feeble perfon among their tribes. Egypt was glad when they departed; for the fear of them fell upon them."

I proceed to confider the difficulty arifing from the command which Jehovah gave to the children of Ifrael, to deftroy the inhabitants of Canaan. This objection has been accounted the moft fpecious of any that has been brought againft the divine original of the Bible; and has been much infifted on by deifts. They have confidently affirmed, that the Ifraelites could have no juft authority to go into Canaan, cut off its inhabitants by the fword, and take poffeffion of their country; and that if it be admitted that the Ifraelites had righteoufnefs on their fide, in thus treating a people at peace with them, it will follow that any nation may deprive another of all that is dear to them as men, without violating the law of benevolence. The enemies of divine revelation have alfo dwelt much on the command for the *total* excifion of the Canaanites, without refpect to age or fex, as breathing a fpirit of cruelty, and therefore unworthy of God.

I have been the more careful in calling up this objection in its full strength, because of the temporary embarrassment it has occasioned in so many minds, when they have begun to inquire into the authority of the scriptures. To assist in removing the difficulty, let the following things be considered.

1st. The character of the Canaanites, whom the children of Israel were commanded to destroy. From the account given of them in sacred history, it appears that they were gross idolaters, and were addicted to vices of the most enormous kind. They consulted with familiar spirits, and practised the arts of sorcery and witchcraft. There was not a crime that agreed with their unbridled lusts, which they did not sanction by their idolatrous rites. *Even their sons and their daughters they burnt in the fire to their gods.* They lived in the open indulgence of fornication, incest, and the sin of Sodom. They even defiled themselves with the beasts of the field. Hence Jehovah gave the following prohibitory precept to the Israelites, " Defile not yourselves in any of these things; for in all these the nations are defiled which I cast out before you. And the land is defiled: therefore I do visit the iniquity thereof upon it, and the land itself vomitteth out her inhabitants."* I know not whether it be poffible to reprefent a nation in a more odious light, than by the figure of their land *vomitting them out*, as too loathfome to endure on its furface.

2dly. It is evident from the national character of the Canaanites, that they juftly deferved deftruction from the hand of God. His purity and juftice forbid the lafting profperity of a nation of profligates. The Lord did not fuffer the Canaanites to be deftroyed, until they had ripened themfelves for ruin by obftinate wickednefs. Near five hundred years before their conqueft by Jofhua, when God renewed the promife to Abraham, that his feed fhould poffefs their land, he declared that there would be a fufpenfion of the performance until feveral future generations were paffed away; and for the following reafon—*The iniquity of the Amorites is not yet full.*† The righteous Lord did not fuffer them to be cut off till their fins had long cried aloud for vengeance. Hence, he cautions his people, as in Deut. ix. 4. "Speak not thou in thine heart, after that the Lord thy God hath caft them out from before thee, faying, For my righteoufnefs

---

* Deut. xviii. 12. Lev. xviii. † Gen. xv. 16.

the Lord hath brought me in to poſſeſs this land; but for the wickedneſs of theſe nations the Lord doth drive them out from before thee."

3dly. If the Canaanites juſtly deſerved deſtruction from the hand of God, it muſt belong to him to appoint the manner of inflicting it. No one will contend but that the Lord might juſtly have waſted them, both old and young, by ſickneſs, or famine, or have ſunk them by an earthquake; or have deſtroyed them by evils of a ſimilar nature. None can deny that towns and cities have been overthrown in ſuch ways, involving each ſex and every age, without diſcrimination. The heart that murmurs at the providence which orders ſuch events, as being neither conſiſtent with rectitude nor goodneſs, is actuated by the ſpirit of atheiſm.

As the execution of the ſentence againſt the wicked lies wholly in the breaſt of the ſupreme Judge, no reaſon can be aſſigned why He might not employ the arms of the Iſraelites, in cutting off the ancient inhabitants of Canaan. Intelligent creatures are as fully under his direction and control as the material world. Beſides, when the former are uſed as the inſtruments in puniſhing, the tokens of the divine wrath are considered as more explicit and dreadful than when evils come through other channels. When David was directed to choose out of war, famine, or pestilence, the scourge to chastise him for his sin in numbering Israel, he prayed that he might not fall into the hand of man.

4thly. THAT the Israelites were commissioned by Jehovah to destroy the Canaanites, is manifest from their history, after their departure from Egypt to their passing over Jordan. The divine miraculous interpositions in their behalf, establishes their commission beyond all reasonable doubt; when taken in connexion with the promises God made to Abraham, and other patriarchs who descended from him, that the land of Canaan should be given to the posterity of Jacob for an inheritance. From the words of Rahab the harlot, to the two spies whom Joshua sent to Jericho, it appears that the inhabitants of Canaan expected that the Israelites would conquer and possess their country, from the wonders wrought for their defence in the wilderness. Joshua ii. 9—11. " And she said unto the men, I know that the Lord hath given you the land, and that your terror is fallen upon us, and that all the inhabitants of the land faint because of you. For we have heard how the Lord dried up the water of the red sea for you, when ye came out of Egypt; and what ye did unto the two kings of the Amorites that were on the other side Jordan, Sihon and Og, whom ye utterly destroyed. And, as soon as we had heard these things, our hearts did melt, neither did there remain any more courage in any man, because of you: for the Lord your God, he is God in heaven above, and in earth beneath.

No objection can remain against the manner of destroying the Canaanites, after candidly attending to their character and desert, the right of the supreme Judge in appointing the instruments of his vengeance, and the full proof that is furnished in support of the commission given to the Israelites, to cut off those abandoned nations, and to plant themselves in their land.

If any should inquire why the instance we have been considering, may not be plead in favor of the Spaniards in destroying the aborigines of Mexico and Peru, under Cortez and Pizarro, I answer, that it does not appear that those American Indians were equally corrupt with the ancient Canaanites; but on the supposition that they were, the Spaniards never had an immediate grant from the supreme King, of the countries they invaded, nor had they a divine commission to kill or enslave the inhabitants. Those avaricious Europeans could not produce miraculous evidence in support of their claim, or of the war they carried on to acquire the lands and the gold of the natives; therefore they were guilty of robbery and murder. They could not derive the least countenance from the principles that justify the conquest of Canaan by Joshua.

If any should pretend to vindicate the iniquitous traffic in the human species, that has been carried on for three hundred years past, by the command for the excision of the Canaanites, let them support their cause by miracles as striking as those that were wrought in favor of the children of Israel, in the days of Moses and Joshua. Let the men who are exploring the coasts of Africa in quest of slaves, open a passage to go on dry ground through wide and deep waters, and arrest the motions of our planetary system, by stretching out their hands, or lifting up their voice—I say, let them perform these or similar miracles in express support of their design, or let them desist from carrying misery and wretchedness to those shores, as they would avoid the guilt of man-stealing, and of shedding innocent blood.

In the destruction of the Canaanites, solemn warnings were given to the people of Israel, and to all other nations to whom the scriptures are known, against idolatry and vice. Is it not worthy of the holiness, justice and goodness of God to give such warnings to mankind? Did he not display his moral perfections by the deluge, and other judgments recorded in scripture history? The mind of Abraham must have been deeply impressed with a belief in the holy majesty of Jehovah, when early in the morning in which Sodom and Gomorrah were wrapped in flames, he beheld the smoke of the country going up, as the smoke of a furnace. The Lord will make ungodly nations to drink the cup of his wrath. Jere. xxv. 31. " A noise shall come even to the ends of the earth: for the Lord hath a controversy with the nations; he will plead with all flesh; he will give them that are wicked to the sword, saith the Lord."

Having attempted to obviate the foregoing objections, I proceed to introduce a *second* argument in support of the inspiration of the scriptures, taken from the miracles which they narrate. To these, appeals have already been made, but their nature and design deserve a more particular consideration; as well as the principal periods of sacred history in which they were wrought.

A MIRACLE is an event contrary to the laws of nature, or the stated course of divine operation, and is addressed to the external senses of mankind. A miracle is as perfectly within the reach of omnipotence, or is wrought with the same ease, as any other thing that is brought into existence. Should the Almighty now command the sun to rise in the west instead of the east, the event would be miraculous, because it is contrary to what are denominated the laws of nature. If water were to ascend a cataract, it would be a reversion of its common course, and therefore a miracle. The miracles recorded in the scriptures, were perceived by those who were present when they were performed, through the medium of their bodily organs. Thus, the appearances and the voice at Mount Sinai, when the law was given, struck the senses of the Israelites. When Christ walked on the sea of Galilee, his disciples were eye-witnesses. No train of reasoning is necessary to convince the spectators when a miracle is performed. Its sudden, extraordinary nature arrests the attention, like the first appearance of a blazing comet, or the noise of thunder.

The apparent design of miracles is to summon the attention of mankind, to some doctrine or duty, revealed or enjoined by Jehovah; and at the same time to prove that the persons who deliver the truths or the laws, are commissioned by him. When God sends messengers with such credentials, their message is clothed with his authority, and demands our faith and obedience. Miracles, though most striking to those who were present when they were wrought, may be so well attested, as to answer the same general purposes to others down to the end of the world. They were of high and absolute importance in the establishment of the Jewish and Christian dispensations. To this general design may be reduced all the miracles recorded in the Old Testament, and in the New.

We have no reason to expect the renewal of miracles; because the canon of scripture has long since been closed. The precise period in which miracles ceased, I pretend not to determine: But we have no evidence that they were continued beyond the infancy of the christian church.

LET us attend to some of the miracles wrought by Moses. While he was in exile in the land of Midian, where he continued forty years, he led his flock to the back-side of the desert, and came to the mountain of God, even to Horeb. To this humble shepherd the Angel of the Lord appeared, in a flame of fire, out of the midst of a bush; and he looked, and, behold, the bush burned with fire, and was not consumed. As he turned aside to see this great sight, Jehovah called to him out of the midst of the bush, and commanded him to go down into Egypt, to deliver the children of Israel from their cruel bondage, and to conduct them unto the good land that he had promised to give them. Moses discovered great reluctance, at first, in entering on the work assigned him; and urged that his nation would not believe him, but would say, " The LORD hath not appeared unto thee." Jehovah directed him to cast the rod in his hand on the ground. He obeyed; it became a serpent; and he fled from before it. By the same authority, he caught it by the tail, and it again became a rod in his hand. He was next commanded to put his hand into his bosom; and when he took it out it was leprous as snow. He was ordered to put his hand into his bosom again; and on his plucking it out the second time, it was cured, and resumed the same appearance with his other flesh. Convinced by these two signs, as well as by other things, of his duty to undertake in the arduous work of delivering Israel from bondage, he with Aaron his brother, went down into Egypt, in obedience to the divine command. It appears from the history recorded in Exodus, that Moses, after his long exile, had given up the expectation which he had entertained forty years before, of delivering the Israelites, and that they were looking out for no such thing. This greatly strengthens the credibility of the story. On the refusal of Pharaoh to release the Israelites from bondage, according to the demand which Jehovah directed Moses to make, Aaron cast down the rod, which had undergone miraculous changes at Horeb, and it became a serpent, in presence of the Egyptian monarch and his ministers. Other miracles were afterwards wrought; in turning the waters of Egypt into blood, in filling the land with frogs, and with swarms of flies, in the plagues of the hail, and the locusts, in bringing on a thick darkness over the land of three days continuance, and to name no more, in the death of the first born, both of man and beast, through-

out the realm, in one night. Thefe miracles, in connexion with thofe afterwards performed at the red fea, at Mount Sinai, and other places, until the chofen people were put in poffeffion of the land of promife, abundantly eftablifh the infpiration of the Old Teftament. Additional proofs of the fame kind were afforded, from the conqueft of Canaan till the days of the prophet Daniel. When Mofes, a little before his death, was exhorting the children of Ifrael to keep the ftatutes and commandments of the Lord, he reminded them of the extraordinary manner in which God had redeemed them from Egypt, and revealed his will, as high motives for their obedience. He appealed to the figns and wonders which had been fhown and wrought before their nation, in proof that their Almighty Redeemer was the only true God, and that their religion was from him. Deut. iv. 32—40. "For
" afk now of the days that are paft, which
" were before thee, fince the day that God
" created man upon the earth; and afk
" from the one fide of heaven unto the oth-
" er, whether there hath been any fuch
" thing as this great thing is; or hath been
" heard like it? Did ever people hear the
" voice of God fpeaking out of the midft
" of the fire, as thou haft heard, and live?

"Or hath God assayed to go and take him
"a nation from the midst of another nation,
"by temptations, by signs, and by won-
"ders, and by war, and by a mighty hand,
"and by a stretched-out arm, and by great
"terrors, according to all that the Lord
"your God did for you in Egypt before
"your eyes? Unto thee it was shewed, that
"thou mightest know that the Lord he is
"God; there is none else besides him.
"Out of heaven he made thee to hear his
"voice, that he might instruct thee: and
"upon earth he shewed thee his great fire,
"and thou heardest his words out of the
"midst of the fire. And because he loved
"thy fathers, therefore he chose their seed
"after them, and brought thee out in his
"sight with his mighty power out of Egypt;
"to drive out nations from before thee,
"greater and mightier than thou art, to
"bring thee in, to give thee their land for
"an inheritance, as it is this day. Know,
"therefore, this day, and consider it in thine
"heart, that the Lord he is God in heaven
"above, and upon the earth beneath: there
"is none else. Thou shalt keep, therefore,
"his statutes, and his commandments, which
"I command thee this day, that it may go
"well with thee, and with thy children after
"thee, and that thou mayest prolong thy

" days upon the earth, which the Lord thy
" God giveth thee, forever."

WHETHER the magicians, mentioned in Exod. vii. and viii. performed real miracles, is a question which has often been brought up in attending to the miracles of Moses; and has been differently answered by divines of high reputation in the Christian Church.

THOSE who adopt the affirmative side of the foregoing question, admit that the evidence is eventually full and decisive in support of the divine mission of Moses; because that the magicians were early confounded in their contest with him, and were brought to confess that Moses was furnished with divine assistance. My limits will not permit me to enter largely into this subject; I shall only suggest a few reasons against the hypothesis, that the magicians performed real miracles.

1st. IF real miracles are admitted to be wrought on the side of those who are engaged for the support of error and wickedness, as the supposed miracles of the magicians in Egypt were, it will be very difficult to show how miracles do in any case confirm the divine mission of any person, or the divine authority of any scheme of religion. Nicodemus, in the third chapter of John, appears to have spoken not only according to the belief of the Jews, but agreeably to the dictates of the human mind, when he said to Christ, *We know that thou art a teacher come from God; for no man can do these miracles that thou doest except God be with him.*

2dly. Moses discovers no marks of discouragement from any thing that the magicians are supposed to have done, in turning their rods into serpents, water into blood, or in bringing up frogs upon the land. But considering his very great diffidence in undertaking the arduous work to which he was called while in Midian, would he not have been greatly agitated, and have been ready to despond, if he had believed that the magicians were possessed of a power to do miracles? How would he have relied on the sign of changing *his* rod into a serpent, as a proof of his divine commission, as the Lord had told him, if the magicians could also turn *their* rods into serpents?

3dly. Whatever the magicians did, they never went first in performing any wonder; but they in their operations always *followed* Moses. It is certainly much easier to imitate than to take the lead, in any thing either great or rare. Men who compofed an order of fuch antiquity and repute among the heathens, as were the magicians, muft have acquired a dexterity in their art, which far furpaffes any thing that has fallen under our notice.

4thly. It plainly appears to us, even at this diftance of time and place from the fcene in Pharaoh's court, that in two of the three inftances in which the magicians imitated Mofes, they wrought on a much fmaller fcale than he did. When Aaron ftretched out the rod over the waters of Egypt, the Lord caufed their ftreams, rivers, ponds, and all their pools to become blood; and they remained in that ftate feven days. The Egyptians, in that time of diftrefs, opened wells or fprings to procure water to drink. The magicians could have but a fmall quantity of water to operate upon. At the inftant of time when Mofes did his miracle there was no water for them to change, fo much as in veffels of wood or ftone. They might afterwards by their art caufe the water taken from a newly opened fpring or well, to affume the appearance of blood. It is affirmed by fome great naturalifts now living that a fmall quantity of water may be made to appear red like blood, by the efforts of art. In the inftance of the frogs the magicians could do very little; becaufe Mofes had before caufed them to go up from the waters of Egypt, and to cover the land.

5thly. PHARAOH is confidered as more criminal for not letting the Ifraelites depart from their bondage, on account of the figns and wonders which were fhown by Mofes and Aaron, even while the magicians imitated their miracles. As a proof of this we need only advert to what is faid concerning the Egyptian monarch, that *he hardened his heart*, or that *his heart was hardened*. If the magicians did as real miracles as Mofes, how could Pharaoh's guilt have been increafed in holding the children of Ifrael in flavery, againft the light reflected upon his underftanding and confcience by what Mofes did? What evidence could Pharaoh collect from figns, which were performed by thofe who demanded the releafe of the oppreffed people, if his wife men who defigned by their wonderful works to countenance him in his conduct, wrought as real miracles as were performed by Mofes and Aaron? If it fhould be faid that the miracles performed by thefe laft exceeded thofe wrought by the magicians, and therefore Pharaoh was the more criminal in refufing to let Ifrael go, it may be anfwered, that according to this hypothefis, there was divine evidence againft divine evidence; which is abfurd and contradictory. Befides, if Mofes exceeded the magicians for the prefent, while the conteft between them continued, how could Pharaoh determine before the trial clofed, that the latter would not in a future inftance get the victory over the former? While there was room to doubt, the Egyptian monarch could not be blamed for waiting the iffue of the conteft; and confequently his guilt would not have been increafed by the miracles of Mofes, during the performance of counter miracles. There appears to be no way to avoid thefe difficulties, but that of denying that the magicians wrought real miracles.

6thly. PHARAOH never applied to the magicians to take away the plagues while they imitated Mofes; but in every inftance to the latter. He could not be influenced to this conduct by his native inclination or intereft. How can this behaviour of his be accounted for, except on the ground, that he was compelled to believe that Mofes only was endowed with miraculous powers?

7thly. THE magicians are exprefsly faid, in the three inftances in which they imitated Mofes, to have wrought *with their inchant-*

ments. The original word rendered *inchantments,* in Exodus vii. and viii. is derived from a verb which signifies *to hide,* or *conceal,* and the plural noun derived from it, signifies *incantations,* or *charms,* or *juggling tricks;* whereby true appearances are covered, and false ones are imposed on the eyes of the spectators. ' The divine law forbids the use of this art; Levit. xix. 26. " Ye shall not eat any thing with the blood ; *neither shall ye use inchantment,* nor observe times." The servants of Jehovah did not indulge such operations. Even Balaam, when he found himself compelled to bless the people of Israel, instead of cursing them according to the wishes of his heart, " went not as at other times *to seek for inchantments.*"* From the use of inchantments adopted by the magicians in Egypt, it may be fairly concluded that what they did, was performed by the exertion of their art; and that therefore they wrought no miracle.

8thly. When the magicians failed in their attempt to bring forth lice with their inchantments, they said unto Pharaoh *This is the finger of God;* which confession implies that what they had done before was effected by art. It is to be observed that the magi-

---

* Numb. xxiv. 1.

cians do not say, " This is the finger of *the Lord*, or *Jehovah*," in whose name Moses did his miracles; but that, " This is the finger of *God*." The word translated *God*, in this passage, is applicable to any Deity; as we find from the use of it in the scriptures. It may therefore be inferred, that the magicians themselves acknowledged that there was no special interposition of *Deity* in all which they had done.

If the foregoing arguments are well founded, it must appear unnecessary that the sacred historian should have said in a formal manner, that the magicians in Egypt wrought no real miracle; since the same idea is communicated by the words which narrate their operations—" *They did so with their inchantments.*"

The magicians, and kindred orders of men, might do many strange and marvellous things in the days of Moses, and they may now; but we seem not to have any evidence that God hath ever wrought a miracle by their hands. When Baal's prophets in the time of Elijah made an effort to call down fire from heaven upon their altar, they were not able to accomplish their wishes. When the exorcists, mentioned in Acts xix. undertook to cast out evil spirits by invoking the name of Jesus, in connexion with their art, they were dreadfully confounded: ver. 15, 16. "And the evil spirit answered and said, Jesus I know, and Paul I know; but who are ye? And the man in whom the evil spirit was, leaped on them, and overcame them, and prevailed against them, so that they fled out of that house naked and wounded." Antichrist claims the power of working miracles, but those he exhibits, are stiled, in scripture, *lying wonders;* not only because they are designed to establish heresy, but because the facts to which he appeals are not of the miraculous kind: as will fully appear to any one who peruses the legends of the Romish church, together with the writings of the reformers.

Having attended to the case of the magicians, which is the most difficult of the kind recorded in the Bible, I need not pay particular attention to that which is contained in 1 Samuel xxviii. relative to the resurrection of the prophet by the witch of Endor. She is not to be considered as a worker of miracles, if some person, under the cover of the night was substituted by her to announce to Saul his destiny. This would be wholly the effect of art. Nor can she be ranked among the performers of miracles, if, as is most probable, Jehovah interposed and raised Samuel, to deliver to the wicked king of Israel his doom. It is I think, obvious from the history, that while the witch was about to practise the art of divination, the prophet suddenly appeared. If this be admitted as fact, she was in no sense employed as an instrument in producing the miracle.

The last miraculous event in the old Testament history which I shall consider, is the one that was performed in the time of the prophet Elijah: Of this we have a particular account in 1 Kings xviii. That prophet lived in the time when Ahab reigned over Israel; a prince who gave himself up with Jezebel his wife, to idolatry and wickedness, above all who had been raised to the throne before him. A drought of more than three years continuance was sent upon the land, for the wickedness of the king and his people; and was followed by a dreadful famine. The prophet Elijah was commissioned by Jehovah to denounce to Ahab the withholding of the dew and the rain during that gloomy period. Near its close he came out of his retirement by divine command, and went boldly to meet the king, who had been seeking to find the place where the prophet was sheltered, that he might put him to death. "And it came to pass, when Ahab saw Elijah, that Ahab said unto him, art thou he that troubleth Israel? And he answered, I have not troubled Israel, but thou and thy father's house, in that ye have forsaken the commandments of the Lord, and thou hast followed Baalim. Now, therefore, send, and gather to me all Israel unto mount Carmel, and the prophets of Baal four hundred and fifty, and the prophets of the groves four hundred, which eat at Jezebel's table." Ahab assembled the people and the prophets according to desire. "And Elijah came unto all the people, and said, how long halt ye between two opinions, if the Lord be God, follow him: but if Baal, then follow him." The people manifested by their silence, that they had nothing to say against so reasonable a proposal. "Then said Elijah unto the people, I, even I only, remain a prophet of the Lord; but Baal's prophets are four hundred and fifty men. Let them, therefore, give us two bullocks; and let them choose one bullock for themselves, and cut it in pieces, and lay it on wood, and put no fire under; and I will dress the other bullock, and lay it on wood, and put no fire under. And call ye on the name of your gods, and I will call on the name of the Lord; and the god that anſwereth by fire, let him be God. And all the people anſwered and ſaid it is well ſpoken." The prieſts of Baal took the bullock which they choſe, and prepared and laid it on their altar. They cried to their god from morning to evening, but there was neither voice, nor any to anſwer, nor any that regarded. Elijah proceeded to repair the altar of the Lord before all the people. He made a trench about it, and laid on the wood and the bullock in order. He commanded water to be poured upon the burnt-ſacrifice and the wood: This was done three times. " And the water ran about the altar; and he filled the trench alſo with water. And it came to paſs, at the time of the offering of the evening ſacrifice, that Elijah the prophet came near, and ſaid, Lord God of Abraham, Iſaac, and of Iſrael, let it be known this day that thou art God in Iſrael, and that I am thy ſervant, and that I have done all theſe things at thy word. Hear me, O Lord, hear me; that this people may know that thou art the Lord God, and that thou haſt turned their heart back again." The people muſt have waited with anxious deſire to ſee the iſſue—the controverſy decided, whether Jehovah or Baal be the true God.

The suspense was immediately removed after the prayer of Elijah was closed. "The fire of the LORD fell, and consumed the burnt-sacrifice, and the wood, and the stones, and the dust, and licked up the water that was in the trench." The people felt the decision of the controversy—They could not doubt for a moment. "They fell on their faces, and they said, THE LORD, HE IS THE GOD! THE LORD, HE IS THE GOD!" In this instance we behold in a striking manner, the proof which miracles afford that JEHOVAH is the only true God, and that mankind are under the highest obligations to worship and obey him, as required in his word.

I pass to the consideration of some of the miracles recorded in the New Testament.

THE number of miracles performed by Jesus Christ was much greater than those which were done by Moses, or Elijah, or any who came before him. He went about all the cities and villages in the land of Israel, healing every sickness and disease.* "His fame went throughout all Syria; and they brought unto him all sick people that were taken with divers diseases, and torments, and those which were possessed with devils, and those which were lunatic, and those that had

* Matth. ix.

the palfy; and he healed them."† He cured perfons, and that in an inftant, who were deaf, and blind, and dumb, and lame. They immediately recovered their hearing, their fight, their fpeech, and the ufe of their limbs; and remained in a ftate of recovery. He removed completely at once, infirmities which had been of many years ftanding. This is altogether different from curing by the application of medicine; which is very flow in its progrefs in overcoming chronic diforders. Chrift reftored foundnefs to the body, as well as regularity to the mind, by uttering a word. Many fuch miracles as the foregoing were performed in a public manner, and before enemies. He fed four thoufand men, befide women and children, with feven loaves of bread, and a few little fifhes; and feven bafkets of fragments remained. At another time he fed about five thoufand men with five loaves and two fifhes; and twelve bafkets of fragments remained. He filenced the tempeft by his voice, and he walked on the waves of the fea. He reftored life to the dead. Three inftances are particularly mentioned, viz. the widow's fon at Nain, Jairus's daughter at Capernaum, and Lazarus at Bethany. Let us

† Matth. iv. 24.

bestow our attention for a moment on these instances.

When Jesus approached the gate of the city of Nain, with many of his disciples and much people, he met a funeral procession. A croud had collected to mourn with a sorrowful mother, in a state of widowhood, whose only son had fallen a victim to death in the bloom of youth: the corpse was now moving to the land of silence. The compassion of Jesus was tenderly touched, as he beheld the flowing tears of a solitary widow, mourning for her only son. "He said unto her, weep not. And he came and touched the bier; and they that bare him stood still." The attention of the throng must have been fixed upon this stranger—Their eyes and their ears were open—What doth this traveller design! The multitude soon heard and saw with amazement—He spoke with an audible voice, *Young man! I say unto thee, Arise!* " And he that was dead sat up, and began to speak. And he delivered him to his mother." The spectators felt a solemn awe; " and they glorified God, saying, that a great prophet is risen up among us; and, that God hath visited his people."*

* Luke vii.

Jairus, a ruler of the synagogue, had one only daughter, about twelve years of age, who lay a dying. He came to Jesus, who was then surrounded by a multitude, and fell at his feet, and with all the distress and anguish which a father feels, when his child appears to be in the agonies of death, besought him to go to his house to stay the departing spirit. As the great physician did not repair to the place so soon as requested, word was soon brought him that the maiden was dead, and that he needed not make the visit lately requested. But when Jesus heard it, he told the messenger, that she should be made whole. He went to the melancholy house, and found the family weeping and bewailing their dead friend. "He took her by the hand, and called, saying, *Maid! arise!* And her spirit came again, and she arose straightway."*

Lazarus of Bethany, was raised from the dead after he had lain in the grave four days. This miracle was wrought in presence of a great number of spectators. They heard the commanding voice of the Son of God, *Lazarus, come forth!* They saw him coming forth from the grave. Some who were present believed on Jesus as the prom-

* Luke viii.

ised Messiah ; but others went their ways to the Pharisees, and made them acquainted with the miraculous event. Whereupon the Jewish council was assembled; the members of which said to each other " What do we ? for this man doeth many miracles. If we let him thus alone, all men will believe on him ; and the Romans shall come and take away both our place and nation.—From that day forth, they took counsel together for to put him to death."*

The resurrection of Jesus Christ, is a miracle, which taken in all its circumstances, is the most remarkable of any that was ever wrought in our world, and furnishes the highest evidence of his divine mission, and that the gospel is from God. Jesus showed unto his disciples while he was pursuing his public ministry, that he must go up to Jerusalem, be delivered into the hands of men, suffer many things of the elders, and chief priests and scribes, and be killed, and be raised again the third day.†

Had not Jesus Christ risen from the dead, his religion must have early perished. Its fate would have been the same with that of the French prophets, a set of enthusiasts who

---

* John xi. † Matth. xvi. 21. Mark ix. 31.

appeared in England about a hundred years ago. When one of their chiefs lay on his death-bed, and was actually expiring, he told his followers round him that he should rise on a certain day and hour; and that if he failed, they must conclude that they had been deluded. The day came—a vast number of people assembled round the grave—as the hour approached, a noted partisan lifted up his voice, and called to his deceased friend—Rise! Oh rise! or we are undone! But the clods continued to cover the dead body, and the delusion was detected in the eyes of the world. If Christ had not risen, as he predicted, his cause would have sunk. Saith the Apostle Paul in 1 Cor. xv. *If Christ be not risen, then is our preaching vain, and your faith is also vain.*

The death of Jesus was not in private among his friends, but in public among his enemies; by whom he was executed as a malefactor. When he was taken down from the cross, his enemies were fully satisfied that he was dead. Life could not have remained in him after the Roman soldier had thrust the spear into his side. His body was lodged in a sepulchre hewn out of a rock, a stone was rolled unto its door. By Pilate's order a seal was put upon the stone, and a guard of soldiers was placed by it. On the third day, *Behold, there was a great earthquake: for the angel of the Lord descended from heaven, and came and rolled back the stone from the door, and sat upon it. His countenance was like lightening, and his raiment white as snow. And for fear of him the keepers did shake, and became as dead men.* The angel said to the women who came unto the sepulchre, *Jesus who was crucified is not here; for he is risen, as he said. Come, see the place where the Lord lay.**

The women who visited the sepulchre in the morning after Christ arose, did not expect in their setting out to find him alive, for their design was to anoint the dead body with the spices they had prepared. None of the disciples of Christ expected his resurrection. They never could understand during his life how his dying, and to be sure in such ignominy, was reconcileable with his Messiahship. They were slow to believe in the resurrection of Christ, after the event had taken place. The force of evidence alone gained their faith. The appearances of Christ to them were continued at different times and places, when few and many were together, during the course of forty days.

---

* Matth. xxviii.

He was seen of above 500 brethren at once; of whom the greater part remained alive when Paul wrote his first epistle to the church of Corinth; many years after the ascension.

The story of the watch placed at Christ's sepulchre, *That his disciples came and stole him away while they slept*, is full of absurdities. They were hired to tell it by a large sum of money given them by the chief priests and elders of the Jews. Do men need bribing to tell the truth? Does not the design of a bribe always carry in it a wish to conceal facts? Besides, as it is well known that those who slept on guard, were if detected, punished by the Roman laws with death, the soldiers would not have dared to confess themseves asleep when on duty, had not the Jewish rulers agreed to pacify Pilate on their behalf. Had there been the least pretext for the story the soldiers told, the chief priests would have been the first men in Judea to bring the watch to punishment; as that would have given credibility to the account which they strove to propagate. Every thing relative to the conduct of the chief priests in this affair, carries fraud in the face of it, and confirms the truth of Christ's resurrection. Moreover, the testimony given by the watch relative to a fact, which, by their own confession, took place while they were asleep, is of such a nature, as is wholly inadmissible before a court of justice, or by the dictates of common sense. Are men to be credited in affirming a fact, which they declare to have happened at a time when they could have no consciousness of it? Is there an honest man of common understanding upon the globe, who would venture to decide in any thing of consequence on such testimony?

It has been objected to the truth of Christ's resurrection that he did not show himself after his death to his judges, and his enemies in general. To obviate this difficulty, it may be observed, that if Christ after he left the sepulchre had gone into their presence, they probably would, from the malice and blindness they had discovered, have considered the appearance as an idle dream; and have remained as obstinate as they were after the resurrection of Lazarus. But let us suppose that by such an appearance they had all been gained over to the belief of the fact, and had become Christ's disciples, would not the enemies of the gospel have said, that since all the great men in the nation had received it, the whole was a contrived plan, and therefore ought to be given up as a cunningly devised fable?

This objection would have carried much more plausibility in it than any that can now be urged. Christianity did not rise up under the patronage of the powerful and the great. It was left to work its way in the world by its internal evidence, and the gracious aids of its founder. Several persons of learning and note were converted to it in its infancy; among these was Saul of Tarsus; but they became friends to the gospel in a way that gives not the least countenance to the suggestion, that it owed its birth to the wisdom of this world. Christ crucified was to the Jews a stumbling block, and to the Greeks foolishness.

WITHIN a short time after Christ's resurrection, his disciples publicly and boldly proclaimed it in Jerusalem, where he was put to death; and wrought miracles on the ground that he was alive. They went forth and preached this doctrine every where, the Lord working with them, and confirming the word with signs following.

To CONCLUDE, we have decisive evidence from the miracles of Moses and the Prophets, and from those of Jesus Christ, and his Apostles, that all scripture is given by inspiration of God.

DISCOURSE V.

The evidence from the Prophecies considered; several popular objections answered; and the discourses concluded with an improvement.

---

2 TIMOTHY iii. 16.

All scripture is given by inspiration of God, and is profitable for doctrine, for reproof, for correction, for instruction in righteousness.

IN the two last discourses, arguments were introduced to prove the divine inspiration of the scriptures, from the nature of the religion they contain, and the miracles recorded in them. I now proceed to a *third* argument, derived from the fulfilment of their prophecies.

By prophecy is meant, the foretelling of events that are not within the reach of human probability, and of which no knowledge can be obtained beforehand but from God. To look into futurity and discern such events, with the time and circumstances of their coming into existence, is peculiar to the infinite mind. Isaiah xlvi. 9, 10. *Remember the former things of old: for I am God, and there is none else; I am God, and there is none like me; declaring the end from the beginning, and from ancient times the things that are not yet done, saying, My counsel shall stand, and I will do all my pleasure.*

That the scriptures abound with prophecies, will be denied by none who have read them. The prophecies are so interwoven with the sacred writings, as not to be separated. If the predictions were not delivered before the events which they hold up as future, had happened, we must give up the Bible, and consider it as a forgery. But if the prophets were let into the secrets of futurity, as we have abundant evidence from the fulfilment of their predictions, they were immediately enlightened from on high, and the scriptures are demonstrated to be the word of the Lord. It has been often proved that the prophecies respecting the captivity of the Jews in Babylon, the coming of Jesus of Nazareth, the destruction of Jerusalem by the Romans, and many others, were deliverd prior to the events which answer to them. The argument in favor of the divine original of the Bible from prophecy, carries irresistible force, when we reflect on the conduct of providence in fulfilling predictions at the present time, which all will grant were written and published many ages ago. To two prophecies of this kind, I now call your attention.

"I shall begin with the prophecy concerning Ishmael, Abraham's son by Hagar, recorded in Gen. xvi. As that woman was wandering in the wilderness, " The angel " of the Lord said unto her, I will multiply " thy seed exceedingly, that it shall not be " numbered for multitude.—Behold, thou " art with child, and shalt bear a son, and " shalt call his name Ishmael; because the " Lord hath heard thy affliction. And he " will be a wild man; his hand will be a-" gainst every man, and every man's hand " against him: and he shall dwell in the " presence of all his brethren." This prediction principally relates to Ishmael's posterity; but a small part of it, beside his birth, could have any accomplishment in his person. A numerous seed descended from him, which remain to this day. It is said of his descendants, in Gen. xxv. 18. That " they dwelt from Havilah unto Shur, that is before Egypt, as thou goest towards Assyria." The place here assigned to them is the same with what was afterwards in scripture called *Arabia*, and continues to have the same name, and to be possessed by the same people, to the present time. The Arabians have never been conquered either by the Assyrians, Persians, Greeks, Romans, Tartars, or any other nation. They have always been a pest to mankind, and have practised robberies upon them. Their hand has been against every man, and of course, every man's hand has been against them, but none have been able to conquer them. They have lived in the midst of all their brethren. In the earlier periods of their history, the descendants of Abraham by Keturah, and the posterity of Isaac bordered upon them. To whatever power these neighbours, or others, rose, they retained their dominion; and were not driven from any part of their territories. " They have from " first to last maintained their independency, " and notwithstanding the most powerful " efforts for their destruction, still dwell in " the presence of all their brethren, and in " the presence of all their enemies."*

---

* Newton on the Prophecies, in two Volumes, 9th Edition, p. 25, 26. Vol. 1.

Who but the omniscient God could have foreseen the state of the descendants of Ishmael? Is not the fulfilment of the predictions concerning them a striking proof in support of the divine original of the scriptures?

The prophecies respecting the state of the Jews, which have been fulfilled in the latter ages, and are now fulfilling, are too remarkable to be passed by in silence, when attending to the present subject. The dispersion and the wretchedness of that people were foretold by Moses. The curses which should fall upon them for their disobedience, are particularly and largely denounced in Deut. xxviii. I shall select a few passages only; ver. 37. *And thou shalt become an astonishment, a proverb, and a by-word, among all nations whither the Lord thy God shall lead thee.* Verses 64, 65, 66. *And the Lord shall scatter thee among all people, from the one end of the earth unto the other; and there thou shalt serve other gods, which neither thou nor thy fathers have known, even wood and stone. And among these nations shalt thou find no ease, neither shall the sole of thy foot have rest; but the Lord will give thee there a trembling heart, and failing of eyes, and sorrow of mind: And thy life shall hang in doubt before thee; and thou shalt fear day and night, and shalt have none assurance of thy life.* These predictions were in a degree fulfilled by the captivity of the kingdoms of Israel and Judah, by the Assyrians and Chaldeans; but have received a fuller accomplishment in the destruction of Jerusalem by the Romans, and in the present dispersion of the Jews. These last events were foretold by Jesus Christ, in Luke xxi. 24. *And they shall fall by the edge of the sword, and shall be led away captive into all nations: and Jerusalem shall be trodden down of the Gentiles, until the times of the Gentiles be fulfilled.*

The Jews were slaughtered in immense numbers, when their city was taken by Titus the Roman general. A vast multitude has perished since, by massacres and persecutions. The Jews have not been permitted to possess the land of Canaan or Palestine, for more than 1700 years; and they are scattered through Asia, and through most of the countries of Europe and Africa; they are found on the American continent, and its adjacent islands. Their land has passed from one set of conquerors to another, and is now in the hands of the Turks; and remains in a low and wretched state. The Jews since their last dispersion have, for the most part, found no rest; but the

Lord has given them *a trembling heart, and failing of eyes, and sorrow of mind.* They have not enjoyed the rights of other citizens in the places where they have lived, they have been banished from many kingdoms; and in not a few instances, government has laid its hand on the property of that unhappy people, in a way of fine and confiscation. They have been detested by the nations, and have been *a by-word* among them. However criminal the Jews may have been, the benevolent heart is pained by even a summary recital of their sufferings, and is rejoiced at the milder treatment they have met with of late. We hope that the period is at hand when their calamities will cease, by the universally opening a door for their enjoyment of freedom, as is done by the spirit of the civil constitution of the United States of America; and above all by their union with the Gentiles throughout the world under the Messiah.

It is remarkable that the Jews, tho' they have met with such hardships and cruelties, yet remain a distinct people. This is the Lord's doing; and verifies what was spoken long ago by the prophets. I shall only mention in this place a passage recorded in Jerem. xxx. 11. addressed to Israel, *For I am with thee, saith the Lord, to save thee: though I make a full end of all nations whither I have scattered thee, yet will I not make a full end of thee; but I will correct thee in measure, and will not leave thee altogether unpunished.* The Jews have not, like other nations, been swallowed up and lost in conquests, by intermingling with their conquerors, or with those among whom they have lived. Tho' they have had the strongest inducements to intermarry, and to blend in all respects, with the Gentiles, they, as a body, remain as widely separated from them by blood and religion as ever. However, they have, in some instances, externally complied with the idolatrous rites of the Romish church, to avoid the cruelties of the court of inquisition, they have at the same time adhered to the faith of their ancestors; and when they have escaped from the danger of the rack, they have renounced christianity in every form, and openly returned to their religion. They remain to this day a striking proof that the author of the prophecies respecting them is divine; and consequently that the scriptures are given by inspiration of God.

Would our limits permit, we might point to the fulfilment of many prophecies, which were delivered long before the events they predict were brought into exiftence. Babylon now lies in ruins, "a poffeffion for the bittern, and pools of water." Tyre, once "a mart of nations," is made "like the top of a rock; a place for the fpreading of nets in the midft of the fea." We behold the man of fin, whofe rife was predicted in the prophecies of the Old and New Teftament, "fitting in the temple of God, fhewing himfelf that he is God; whofe coming is after the working of Satan, with all power, and figns, and lying wonders." And, to name no more, we behold now fulfilling the prophecy recorded in Revelation xvii. 16. "And the ten horns which thou fawelt upon the beaft, thefe fhall hate the whore, and fhall make her defolate, and naked, and fhall eat her flefh, and burn her with fire." The European kingdom which lead the way in giving temporal dominion to the beaft revived under the antichriftian tyranny, is now feizing on the wealth and deftroying the influence which fhe once gloried in giving to the Roman Pontiff. We are furnifhed with abundant proof, that the pens of the prophets were guided by Him who, from eternity, beholds all the events of time. The nearer we approach to the end of the world, the evidence in fupport of the infpiration of the Bible from the fulfilment of the prophecies, becomes more and more clear and convincing. Whatever abuses are made of the increasing light by the wicked, " the wise shall understand."

My designed brevity on the copious subject of these discourses, forbids me to add to the foregoing arguments. I shall, after noticing a few popular objections, conclude with a practical improvement.

Some have attempted to countenance their dislike of the scriptures, by saying, that the language adopted in some parts of those writings, particularly in certain passages in the Old Testament, puts modesty to the blush.

Persons of much information will not be perplexed with this difficulty. It will at once occur to them, that when God speaks to any part of the human race, he must address them in a language which they understand, or the design of revelation will be lost. It must follow of course, that the language of the age and the place when and where the revelation is made, must be adopted. The meaning of particular words is constantly altering by usage. The word *knave*, for instance, in our language, was heretofore understood to mean a *diligent servant;*

but cuſtom now appropriates it to one who is guilty of *fraud* in his dealings with mankind. Cuſtom is as much the ſtandard of decency in the clothing of our thoughts, as in the clothing of our bodies. Some of the words and phraſes in our tranſlation of the Bible, which may appear indelicate when compared with modern ſtyle, did not offend againſt delicacy two hundred years ago; and they may not two hundred years hence, or in a much ſhorter term. Among a civilized people it is as eaſy to diſcern a rotation in words and phraſes, as in any thing elſe that is equally under human control. It would be very ſtrange indeed, if the original language of the pentateuch, which was committed to writing more than three thouſand years ago, perfectly ſuited the various taſtes which have prevailed in ſtyle, from the days ot Moſes to our time. It is to be remarked that the books which he wrote have paſſed through very different ſtates of ſociety, in the lapſe of ſo many ages; to each of which it is impoſſible that they ſhould be compleatly conformed: Yet the manner in which thoſe books were written will abide the teſt of ſound criticiſm at the preſent era of high literary improvement.

Let us admit, for a moment, that the whole phraseology and manner of writing in the most ancient parts of the Jewish scriptures, perfectly corresponded with modern taste—I say, let us make this supposition, in order to learn whether that part of the Bible which is accused of indelicacy, would be as defensible as it now is. We may discern at once the effect of the supposed change. The men who cavil now, would immediately tack about, and exclaim against the pentateuch as a forgery, from its style. Hence, we see that the antiquity of the style used in the Mosaic writings, as well as in other parts of scripture, is a matter of importance in the controversy with infidels. It was as proper that the sacred penmen should adopt the language and manner of writing peculiar to their own times, as that in alluding to mountains in their discourses to the Jews, they should name *Horeb, Carmel, or Hermon,* rather than the *Allegany,* or the *Andes.* After what has been said on the change of the meaning of words and the state of society, it is evident that no one has any just cause to impeach the language of the scriptures of offences against modesty.

The disputes about what the religion of the Bible is, among those who profess to adopt it, have been urged by some as an objection against its divine original. To this it may be answered,

1st. That the enemies of divine revelation are not agreed among themselves. Some infidels profess to believe that God is a good being; others deny that any such conclusion can be formed. Some of them consider the soul of man as immortal; whilst others suppose that it dies with the body. If the disputes among christians overthrow christianity, the disputes among deists overthrow deism. The objection weighs nothing on either side, and is wholly impertinent.

2dly. A considerable number of the controversies among christians do not respect the essentials of their religion; but are to be accounted for from the manner in which they are educated, the religious treatises they read, the persons with whom they associate in the early periods of serious thoughtfulness, and similar causes. Differences of this kind do not prove that the Bible inculcates opposite principles; for it is admitted that they do not materially affect what is necessary to fit men for everlasting happiness.

3dly. It is granted that opinions have been maintained by some who profess to believe in the inspiration of the scriptures, which strike at their fundamental truths. But the rise of damnable heresies is so far from overthrowing the Bible, that it confirms it; for that book contains many predictions that such errors will appear; especially in the last days.

Violent prejudices have been conceived against the religion of Jesus Christ, from the bad things which have been done under the cloak of it. To remove this stumbling block, let it be observed,

1st. That if the bad things which have been done by those who call themselves christians, go to the subversion of the gospel, deism must be overthrown according to the same plan of reasoning. I presume that no one who is the most warmly engaged in support of infidelity, will affirm that all deists have shown high reverence to the Deity in their behaviour, or that they have all been men of sobriety, justice, mercy and truth. We have to acknowledge with grief, that many abominable things have been done by persons who have called themselves the disciples of Jesus Christ; but if we must give up our religion on account of their conduct, the deists must give up theirs on account of the impious and debauched morals of some of their order.

2dly. There is nothing in the nature of revealed religion which tends to the corruption of morals; but every thing in it tends to make bad men better. The moral law requires holiness, and forbids every sin. The gospel breathes the same spirit. It promises pardon and happiness only to the penitent, and encourages with the hope of a crown of righteousness, patient continuance in well doing. The punishments threatened to the wicked are suited to alarm them, and to deter from the practice of iniquity. The religion of Jesus Christ has actually had the happiest influence on those who have cordially embraced it; as has appeared from their lives and deaths.

3dly. Wicked men would not cloak their wickedness under the garb of the christian profession, unless there were something in the gospel which recommends it to the consciences of mankind. There could be no counterfeit coin, if there were no real coin. Men do not counterfeit iron or lead; but silver and gold, or something that represents the value of these precious metals. Those persons who commit iniquity under the mask of friendship to the gospel, are so far from proving it to be of no worth, that even they themselves by implication, testify in its favor, though it is against their lusts.

4thly. We ought not to conclude against the worth of the christian religion from its abuses, on account of the absurdities which such an inference will draw after it. We must, to be consistent with such a conclusion, pronounce all the blessings of common providence to be evils in themselves; for they all have been, and still are, shamefully abused. If we pronounce every thing bad, and to be avoided, which has been employed for a bad purpose, we must consider as evil, food and raiment, the ground on which we tread, the streams that water it, the produce of the garden and the field, the light which strikes our eyes, and the air we breathe. We need not wonder that persons who dispute against the goodness of God, from the pains they bring upon themselves by abusing it, wish to take refuge in annihilation, and indulge the forlorn hope that by suicide they shall hasten their return to the womb of nothing.

5thly. It will be acknowledged by every candid observer, that the religion of the gospel promotes social happiness in every circle in which it reigns. It prevents the wretchedness which flows from riot and debauchery, suppresses the malignant passions, and diffuses the calm and pure pleasures of temperance, diligence, contentment, and friendship. Whatever persecutions have been endured for righteousness' sake, it is too plain to be denied, that the practice of christianity gives a happiness to individuals and to collective bodies, to which those are strangers who treat it with contempt. It has moreover been abundantly demonstrated by able writers, that where it is externally regarded by the inhabitants of a country in general, their morals are not so loose as are those of nations devoted to pagan idolatry.

It is hoped that the observations which have been made, will be thought sufficient to wipe away the reproach which has been cast upon the christian religion, from the bad things that have been done by its hypocritical professors.

Those who reject the divine authority of the Bible, have endeavored to justify their unbelief, by pleading, that they cannot be under obligations to conform their faith and practice to a book, which contains mysteries above the comprehension of the human mind.

If the objections of this kind are juſt, it will follow that we are not bound to believe any thing which we cannot comprehend. But is there a man on the earth, "in his right mind," who will avow this conſequence? We are unable to comprehend the works of nature with which we are ſurrounded. We know not how water is congealed into the hardneſs of ſtone; nor can we comprehend the growth of even a ſingle blade of graſs. Man is a myſtery to himſelf. He cannot tell why certain kinds of food nouriſh his body rather than others; nor how his limbs are put in motion by the volitions of his ſoul. If we are not bound to give our aſſent to any thing which we cannot underſtand in all its parts, we muſt deny facts which are daily taking place before our eyes, yea more, we muſt deny our own exiſtence. The objection we are now conſidering will go to atheiſm; for no creature can fathom abſolute eternity. If there be a God he never had a beginning. When the human mind contemplates this ſubject it is ſwallowed up and loſt. "Canſt thou by ſearching find out God? Canſt thou find out the Almighty unto perfection?"

In the ſupernatural revelation God hath

made of his will, he fpeaks like himfelf—a Being infinitely great. Were all the myfteries which are delivered in the facred volume, perfectly on a level with our limited minds lately called into exiftence, the government of the moral world would be placed in a lower grade than the kingdom of nature, and we fhould not have the fame evidence as we now have that the finger of God is imprinted on the fcriptures. But tho' fome of the doctrines of the Bible are fo high that we can know but little concerning them in this dark probationary ftate, they can be fufficiently apprehended even by babes in underftanding to obtain eternal life. Befides, the truths which are moft myfterious are fo interwoven with thofe which are plain, that if we reject the former, we muft reject the latter. The various parts of this remarkable book form one harmonious fyftem of faith and practice.

The laft objection that I fhall notice is taken from the fmall extent within which the writings of the Old and New Teftament have been known. Since the fcriptures exhibit an exclufive claim of guiding the human race in the way of truth and happinefs, it is contended, that their partial fpread is inconfiftent with the character of Him who is the Father of all mankind, and is no respecter of persons; and that therefore they cannot be given by inspiration of God. To obviate this objection, let the following things be considered,

1st. God in his common providence distributes his gifts, both of body and mind, very variously; as daily experience teaches. It will not be pretended that men have just cause to complain of him, because he bestows upon some a more vigorous animal frame, or a higher degree of intellect, than upon others. No reason can be assigned, why the means of moral and religious improvement may not be as greatly diversified, by the sovereign of the universe, as other blessings are. Besides, the obligation derived from privileges, is proportioned to their nature and degree. Mankind are not punished for disregarding truths of which they could have no knowledge; but for resisting the light that has shone before them.

2dly. Since the whole human race have forfeited every favor from the hand of God, by sin, he may justly exclude them all from happiness, and consequently may deny them opportunity of becoming acquainted with those writings which contain the words of eternal life. All the favors enjoyed by apostate creatures, flow from divine sovereign mercy; which excludes every idea of claim on their part. Those, therefore, who are left in heathenish darkness, experience no injustice. Their demerit is not lessened, nor is their state rendered any more deplorable, by reason of God's conduct in giving the scriptures to others. If any refuse to receive them because they are not known throughout the world, they discover great ingratitude, and perverseness. God has conferred upon us, the inhabitants of the United States of America, a larger portion of freedom than is possessed by most nations. Shall we murmur, and throw away our liberties, because providence has not caused all our fellow-men to enjoy the same blessings? Who hath licensed a worm of the dust to dictate to the sovereign Ruler of heaven and earth! Or to say unto him, "What doest thou!"

3dly. It is owing to the criminal indifference of mankind to the scriptures, that the knowledge of them is confined within such narrow limits. Had, for instance, the several families of the sons of Noah, in their dispersions from the plain in the land of Shinar, been friends to the truths which had at that time been revealed, they would have faithfully preserved them, and made high exertions to transmit them to their posterity. Had the word of the Lord been sweet unto their taste, they would have been much more desirous of handing it down to their successors, than they were their knowledge of the arts. A like pious zeal passing from one generation to another, would have prevented the ignorance of divine revelation which soon prevailed. By the time of Abraham there was a general departure to idolatry. That renowned patriarch sojourned in many places, after he left Ur of the Chaldees in obedience to the command of God; for the setting up his worship in a pure form. But the people among whom he resided, in Canaan, in Egypt, and in other countries, did not improve the opportunity of learning from him the truths and laws which he had immediately communicated to him from God, or had been transmitted to him through the preceding inspired men. The Egyptians paid no lasting attention to the mighty works wrought among them by the arm of Jehovah, in the days of Moses; nor did they regard the means of instruction in the knowledge of the revealed will of God, to which they might have had access. When the Israelites were settled in Canaan, they were placed in the central spot of the then-known world. On different sides of them lay Egypt, Arabia, Syria, Chaldea, and Assyria; out of which nations arose the first empires of note among mankind. Under those monarchies the arts and sciences were first cultivated, and from them have been spread among the inhabitants of the western regions. The land given to the children of Israel is washed on one side by the Mediterranean sea, and bordered on the once famous cities of Tyre and Sidon; which extended their commerce to distant countries. To the nations of the east the chosen people were well known, whilst they dwelt in Canaan. By their captivity under the Assyrians and Chaldeans, the sacred books were carried into many parts of Asia; where they were kept by the dispersed Jews until the day when the Messiah appeared. In the ages which followed the return of some of the captives to Jerusalem under Cyrus, and the rebuilding of their city and temple, the Jews became well known to the Greeks and the Romans. The Apostles in their time carried the gospel far beyond the bounds of Judea, and preached the word of eternal life among the Gentiles.

If there had been a general love of divine truth among the human race, the scriptures would have been disseminated far and wide on this inhabited globe. From the inattention to the inspired writings which has appeared in the conduct of mankind, it is manifest that they have not chosen to retain God in their knowledge. Instead of charging him with an unjust partiality, let them confess that sin is the cause of the extensive reign of heathen darkness. It is wholly owing to the mere sovereign mercy of God, that the knowledge of divine revelation has not perished from the earth.

Having taken a brief view of some of the principal arguments in support of the truth and inspiration of the Bible, and attempted to obviate several objections, I proceed to improve the subject.

1. We may reflect on the unreasonable and dangerous conduct of those who are endeavoring to undermine, and destroy the influence of revealed religion; by representing it as the work of visionary or interested men. Many of the deists have never given themselves the trouble of examining into the evidences of the truth and inspiration of the scriptures; but having picked up here and there something which they dislike in them, either by desultory reading, or from promiscuous company, they proceed to assert

with great confidence, that those writings are the work of a mercenary priesthood, or designing politicians. Such treatment of a book which claims a divine origin, not only announces the badness of their hearts who thus hastily reject it, but does no honor to their understandings. Among the few infidels who have gone into elaborate disquisitions concerning the authority of the scriptures, methods have been adopted, by men of genius and science, to overthrow those writings, which carry in them the grossest absurdities. If the same kind of reasoning were employed on any other subject, they themselves would look upon it with contempt. For the sake of evading the evidence from miracles, deists have labored to establish such rules, for determining the existence of facts of which we have not been personal witnesses, as would destroy our faith in all history. They have fallen into errors of the most palpable kind, in their attempts to prove that the Bible is at variance with itself. As, for instance, when the different writers of any part of its history, do not say precisely the same thing, or one of them mentions facts omitted by another, infidels reject the whole as the contradictory accounts of lying imposters. At the same time they will give full credit to many authors of civil hiſtory, who, in narrating the ſame general events, mention different circumſtances from each other, and will ſpeak of ſuch hiſtorians with applauſe. Deiſts will grant that God may deſtroy countries by the peſtilence, famine, or earthquakes; but if he employ men as the inſtruments of his wrath, as he did in cutting off the inhabitants of Canaan, they cry out, *cruelty! horrid* cruelty! They overlook the proof of the inſpiration of the ſcriptures, which is furniſhed by miracles of the moſt ſtriking kind. They ſhut their eyes againſt the light that ſhines with meridian brightneſs, in the fulfilment of the prophecies. They withhold no exertions, in their power, to heap reproach upon that pure and benevolent religion, which correſponds with the divine character, opens a door of hope to the guilty, and conducts the humble and the penitent to a world of everlaſting joy. The open enemies of the goſpel, ſtrive to bring into univerſal contempt the only religion that can reconcile mankind to God, and unite them in permanent love to one another. Infidels themſelves are very much indebted, for their ſpeculative knowledge of the Deity and moral virtue, to the Bible. By rejecting it they diſcover their ingratitude, and ſhort ſightedneſs.

WHAT advantages do deists expect to derive from trampling under foot the holy scriptures? They have nothing to put in the place of the doctrines which they explode, that can yield them solid enjoyment in their gayest seasons. What consolation can their principles afford, when carried into practice, in days of trouble, or in the hour of serious reflection? Their philosophy cannot alleviate their pains; by assuring them of a future state, or by pointing out the road which leads to substantial interminable happiness. But do they wish to rid themselves of the belief of a future state of rewards and punishments? and hope to die like the brutes? Wonderful sagacity! What! do the honor and happiness of man stand on a level with the honor and happiness of the beasts of the field!

WHAT benefit will society derive from the spread of deistical principles? Have they ever when fully imbibed, reformed a single vicious person? Experience demonstrates that in proportion as they prevail among a people, they weaken reverence towards the name of God, and are accompanied with loose morals. Such are the unhappy effects which infidelity produces: nor can they be denied on account of the regular lives of a few of its friends, who are immersed in study, or whose high official rank impels to pay a decent respect to the general opinion. Civil laws will be found feeble restraints on communities, when the restraints of revealed religion are destroyed.

Those who make a direct attack on the sacred volume are highly criminal. Nothing can justify them in acting against the light that is held up before them, in the word and works of God. None are required to believe the scriptures without sufficient evidence to satisfy the rational mind; but since they are abundantly supported by the scheme of religion they contain, as well as by external testimonies, none can deny their divine original without incurring infinite guilt. The difficulties that have been started relative to their history, their faith and morals, may be removed to the satisfaction of the candid. It is impious in creatures to suggest that a better manifestation of truth might have been made than is exhibited in them. There is a depth in God's wisdom and knowledge which we cannot fathom. He only knows how to display his perfections before finite intelligencies in the best manner to glorify his holy name, and what are the most suitable means to bring sinners to repentance. A cavilling temper is never satisfied. If any will not hear Moses and the Prophets, Christ, and the Apostles, neither would they be persuaded tho' one rose from the dead.

WHAT confusion would fill the mind of a deist, should one of his converts address him in the moment of remorse, " You, Sir, " first taught me to laugh at religion—then " to doubt its truth—and then to trample " it under foot. I followed you next into " vice—I threw off restraint—I have not " feared God, nor have I regarded man. " I tremble to think of my end: For tho' " I still wish to disbelieve, my conscience " whispers—*what if the gospel I have denied* " *should prove true at last!*" How, O ye sons of infidelity! who boast of making disciples to your creed, and to every fashionable vice—how can ye endure to meet the souls you have deluded and undone, at the bar of God! They will rise as swift witnesses against you before him who will judge the world in righteousness. Be entreated to read the scriptures with a candid, serious temper, and impartially examine the arguments which establish their truth and inspiration. God grant that you may no longer remain enemies of the Gospel; but that it may be rendered effectual to your salvation.

2. In a review of the subject of these discourses, we are taught the duty of the friends of revealed religion, to labor for its defence, and to make it the guide of their lives.

We declare with our lips our belief in the truth and inspiration of the scriptures of the Old and New Testament, and that the enjoyment of them is a privilege of inestimable worth. We profess a high veneration for these writings; because they contain a rich and inexhaustible treasure of divine knowledge, and because they point out the only way to escape everlasting misery, and to obtain eternal life. We cannot testify our gratitude for having the oracles of God committed unto us, if we do not search into their meaning with diligence, and listen to them with a humble and devout frame of mind. The man of real piety, delights in the law of the Lord, and in it doth he meditate day and night. He crieth after knowledge, and lifteth up his voice for understanding; he seeketh her as silver, and searcheth for her as for hidden treasures. It is surprising to find in some persons of mature age and good abilities, among the professed friends of the Bible, but a small acquaintance with its history or doctrines. Instead of attending to the word of the Lord their minds are swallowed up in worldly pursuits, or are diverted from the study of it, by books of wit and humour.

MANY of the difficulties which occur in the reading of the scriptures, will be removed by comparing one passage with another, relative to the same subject in different parts of those writings. The doctrines which they contain that far surpass our comprehension, cannot be eradicated without giving up the sacred volume into the hands of its avowed enemies, and placing it on the same ground with the works of a heathen Plato, or Seneca. Those who humbly wait on God will be guided into all necessary truths : " The meek will he guide in judgment ; and the meek will he teach his way." Believers will be kept by the power of God through faith unto salvation.

THERE is reason to expect from present appearances, and from the prophecies, that the church will meet with violent assaults from infidelity, between the period in which we live, and the time when " the earth shall be full of the knowledge of the Lord, as the waters cover the sea." Now, when the enemy is coming in like a flood, we are loudly called upon to lift up a standard against him. The performance of this duty, requires our attention to the arguments which demonstrate the scriptures to be true, and from God; and our earnest endeavors to maintain the faith which was once delivered unto the saints. Christian teachers are under a peculiar and solemn charge, to continue in the things which they have learned of Jesus Christ; and to labor to impress the belief on the minds of others, that *all scripture is given by inspiration of God, and is profitable for doctrine, for reproof, for correction, for instruction in righteousness.* Above all, let every friend of revealed religion imbibe its spirit, and obey its laws. If we love the word of the Lord, we shall place a high value on the sabbath, and on all divine institutions: And shall bear testimony against the various courses which dishonor God, and tend to destroy mankind. Let parents teach their children the doctrines and duties of christianity, and enforce their instructions by a holy example.

DOTH the gospel point out immortality to man, let this solemnize our minds, and incite us to give diligence to make our calling and election sure. Nothing can counterbalance the loss of the soul. What are all the pleasures, the riches, and the honors of the world, when compared with " an inheritance incorruptible, and undefiled, and that fadeth not away!" Let us remember that the grace of God which bringeth salvation, " teacheth us, that denying ungodliness and worldly lusts, we should live soberly, righteously, and godly, in this present world; looking for that blessed hope, and the glorious appearing of the great God and our Saviour Jesus Christ."

3. I shall conclude these discourses with an address to the rising generation.

Dear Youth,

You are coming into active life in a day very different, in several respects, from any former period. The late revolution in our country has extended its influence far and wide; and appears designed by providence to draw after it a train of consequences, whose importance rises to a height that baffles the calculations of the human mind. We are bound to give thanks to God for the rare privilege we enjoy of discussing every subject as publicly as we please, and of expressing our sentiments without restraint. It is a melancholy thought that when so wide a door is opened for the spreading of truth, error and wickedness prevail. Popery and superstition have received a deep wound; at the same time infidelity lifts up its head, and open vices make swift and alarming progress. The heart of man is the same now as it ever has been since the apostacy; but it shows itself in a different form from what it has usually done among christian nations, and calls in principles to justify its criminal indulgencies with more confidence than had before been seen. Many in our day give out that the age of reason is come, and that mankind may now determine for themselves what is virtue and what is vice, without any regard to the scriptures. They seem to think themselves at full liberty, in the sight of God, to reject any revelation he may make, without incurrring his displeasure. If our choice be the only rule of conduct that is binding upon us, we are placed in a lawless universe, and are not accountable to God.

PAUSE a moment—and reflect on the evil and danger of being led astray by opinions which flatter the pride of the heart, and are an inlet to every vice. If you regard your own peace and safety, you will not listen to men who set their mouth against the heavens, and advocate the cause of licentiousness.

Look on the effects of infidelity upon those who are scoffing at the Bible, and are striving to influence others to treat it with contempt. Do they appear to have the fear of God before their eyes? Can you believe that their real aim is to promote your true happiness? A sense of propriety, must render a set of low characters disgusting to you, who belch out their hatred of religion in the noisy clubs, where serious thoughtfulness is banished, and where ardent spirits animate the blustering hero of the night. Pity the poor creature who curses the book which forewarns him of his awful fate, and commands him to lead a life of temperance and sobriety. From persons of a different description you are in much greater danger of being proselyted to infidelity. You may in your intercourse with mankind, meet with deists whose talents are respectable, and whose address is engaging. These will consult your feelings, and will not shock you with a sudden proposal of renouncing the christian faith; but will suggest doubts relative to its historical truth, or the fitness of its doctrines, or the justice of its precepts.

It is not to be expected that those who have been trained up, from their childhood, in the belief of the scriptures, will renounce them at once, and instantly take a leap into the abyss of deism. Persons who make this dreadful plunge, usually advance towards it from small beginnings. You will progress towards the gulph which has swallowed up the avowed enemies of the Bible, if you are in any degree entangled with what goes under the name of *Modern Liberality ;* which affirms, that it is a matter of perfect indifference what sentiments any adopt for their religious creed. It is not pretended by christians, that a mere assent to revealed doctrines forms a good character ; but they cannot be so absurd as to allow that all opinions are alike friendly to virtue. Is it as probable that the man who believes in annihilation at death, will refrain from perjury, as he who believes that he shall exist in another world, and that there God will call him to an account for his conduct in this ? Have we the same reason to look for purity in him who worships a stock or a stone, as in him who worships Jehovah ? Infidels make high professions of liberality, as above defined : But if they speak their real sentiments, why do they make exertions to destroy the faith of others in the Bible ? What cause can they assign for their zeal in proselyting, if they efteem it to be perfectly indifferent what creed any one adopts?

WERE the Bible to perish from among us, there would be no means left, sufficient to prevent paying divine honors to the departed spirits of patriots and heroes, or even to the inanimate creation. The impious, obscene, and cruel rites of paganism would be established, should christianity cease to enlighten us; and our religious state would be the same with that of by far the largest proportion of mankind now on the earth. Human science would not be found a sufficient guard to defend us against such evils; for the learned Greeks and Romans were, at least, as much given to idolatry, as the savages that roam in the desert. The history of the whole heathen world from the days of Abraham until now, exhibits the same melancholy picture with Greece and Rome. A knowledge of the arts and sciences is very useful; but cannot stand in the place of divine revelation.

IF any should plead that the miseries which have flown from corrupt rituals would be avoided by annihilating every form of religion, they suppose a fact which can never generally happen, so long as hope and fear remain in the human breast. But if thee vent they contemplate could be realized, each individual would feel himself licensed to live according to nature, and a scene of wretchedness would ensue, especially in large communities, far surpassing any thing the world has hitherto seen. Neither property, nor chastity, nor life, would be protected; and the earth would groan under the horrors of the infernal regions.

BEWARE, dear youth, of drinking in the poison of infidelity. Embrace the religion which came from above, and make it the guide of your lives. In this choice you will find light, peace, and joy, and will be secured from falling into fatal snares. Joseph, in the bloom of youth and beauty, was protected in a dangerous moment, by reverencing the laws of Jehovah. He replied to the importunate seducer, *How can I do this great wickedness, and sin against God?* Impartially review the evidences of the truth and inspiration of the Bible. If you read this holy book with diligence and meekness, you will be charmed with the pure and benevolent spirit which it breathes; and will be fully persuaded that no being but God can be its author. The miracles recorded in the Old Testament and in the New, and the fulfilment of the prophecies, give a divine sanction to the scriptures.

Trifle not away the morning of life in vain amusements, or in hearkening to fables. You are not creatures of a day; but are born for eternity. The present momentary state will be followed with consequences of infinite importance. Secure without delay the glorious immortality set before you in the gospel. From early life may you know the holy scriptures, which are able to make you wise unto salvation through faith which is in Christ Jesus: To Him be glory for ever and ever. Amen.

www.ingramcontent.com/pod-product-compliance
Lightning Source LLC
Chambersburg PA
CBHW022115160426
43197CB00009B/1034